Young Adult Literature and Spirituality

Young Adult Literature and Spirituality

How to Unlock Deeper Understanding with Class Discussion

William Boerman-Cornell
Deborah Vriend Van Duinen
Kristine Alatheia Mensonides Gritter
Xu Bian

ROWMAN & LITTLEFIELD
Lanham • Boulder • New York • London

Published by Rowman & Littlefield
An imprint of The Rowman & Littlefield Publishing Group, Inc.
4501 Forbes Boulevard, Suite 200, Lanham, Maryland 20706
www.rowman.com
86-90 Paul Street, London EC2A 4NE, United Kingdom

Copyright © 2023 by William Boerman-Cornell, Deborah Vriend Van Duinen, Kristine Alatheia Mensonides Gritter, and Xu Bian

Quotes in chapter 1 are from *Internment* by Samira Ahmed, copyright © 2019.
  Reprinted by permission of Little, Brown and Company, an imprint of Hachette Book Group, Inc.
Quotes in chapter 7 are taken from pages 14, 57, 58, 76, 227, 113 of *The Poet X* by
  Elizabeth Acevedo. Text Copyright 2018 by Elizabeth Acevedo.
Quotes from *Movies Are Prayers* by Josh Larsen, copyright 2017, are used
  with permission.

All rights reserved. No part of this book may be reproduced in any form or by any electronic or mechanical means, including information storage and retrieval systems, without written permission from the publisher, except by a reviewer who may quote passages in a review.

British Library Cataloguing in Publication Information Available

Library of Congress Cataloging-in-Publication Data Available

ISBN 978-1-4758-6209-6 (cloth) | ISBN 978-1-4758-6210-2 (paper) | ISBN 978-1-4758-6211-9 (ebook)

To all our students (who are learning to be teachers) from your teachers (who are still learning to be students) in hopes that, in the midst of all the busy-ness and pressure of teaching and studying, you will grab hold of books with both hands, take a deep breath, and enjoy them with all your might.

Contents

Foreword	ix
Preface	xv
Acknowledgments	xix
Chapter 1: Prayers of Lament in *Internment*	1
Chapter 2: Yearning in *The Hate U Give*	13
Chapter 3: *Speak* and *Long Way Down*: Graphic Novels for Prayers of Anger	23
Chapter 4: Confession in *Goodbye Days*	35
Chapter 5: Seeing Equanimity in *brown girl dreaming*: Using Havruta	51
Chapter 6: Thankfulness in *The War That Saved My Life*	65
Chapter 7: *Louisiana's Way Home* and *The Poet X* as Prayers of Reconciliation	81
Chapter 8: Using Havruta to Consider *Orbiting Jupiter* and *The Beast Player* as Prayers of Obedience	93
Chapter 9: Prayers of Contemplation in *Where the Mountain Meets the Moon*	109
Chapter 10: Finding Joy in *The Fault in Our Stars* through Florilegium	119
Chapter 11: *The Inquisitor's Tale*: Using PaRDeS to Explore Pilgrimage	129
Conclusion: Closing Our Discussion and the Books	147

References	153
Index	157
About the Authors	159

Foreword

Two stories.

Once upon a time, in the first half of the nineteenth century, Rabbi Moshe of Kobryn came to visit his friend, Rabbi Israel of Rizhyn, whom he found at home just before the commencement of the sabbath. Rabbi Israel was smoking his pipe—in fact, the room was filled with the smoke of his pipe—and when Rabbi Moshe entered, Rabbi Israel took the pipe from his lips and greeted Rabbi Moshe with these words:

A man was walking through the darkening woods, lost, with the sabbath just upon him. Fearful of entering into the sabbath lost and cold and without the candles and the prayers—not to say the meal—he was delighted to see a house in the distance. When he reached it, he knocked, and knocked again, and again, and finally entered the house in his desperation. Inside, he saw a fierce robber just rising from out of his sleep, awakened by the man's entrance. Between them was a table, and on the table was a gun, and both rushed for it—and by a miracle, the man almost late for the sabbath reached it first. He grabbed the gun, and as the robber rushed upon him, he thought, *If I hit him, then everything will be all right. And if I miss, then the room will fill with smoke, and I will escape, and everything will still be all right.*

Then the clock in Rabbi Israel's study chimed the hour.

Rabbi Israel put down his pipe, smiled, and quietly said to Rabbi Moshe, "Sabbath!"[1]

I am going to wait to tell the second story. Please be patient.

To understand this tale of Rabbi Israel and Rabbi Moshe, it seems pretty clear that you would have to have some sense of the liturgical and religious life of the Hasidic masters, otherwise the story is absurd—or worse, meaningless. You would need to understand the meaning of the sabbath to comprehend the narrative irony of what the man is encountering. You would need to sense the imperative of the sabbath and its celebration to understand the eagerness of the man who is lost in the woods. You'd need to understand some of the tension he feels beyond the threat of the fierce robber: Can he do the work of pulling the trigger if the sabbath has begun, never mind the act of killing or maiming another? Is even the act of making one's escape a violation of the sabbath, despite the urgency of the moment? And of course, at the center of this story is the image of the table with the gun upon it. Is that meant to be a negative parallel to the sabbath table—here transformed into a table with a life-threatening weapon upon it instead of the life-affirming sabbath meal and candles? Or is the gun, oddly enough, to be seen as a reflection of the sabbath, since the gun may be the means of preserving the man's life?

And why does Rabbi Israel tell Rabbi Moshe this story with its perfectly timed climax—a climactic moment that is halted by the chiming of the clock to announce the sabbath? Is this meant to rebuke Rabbi Moshe for arriving so close to the beginning of the sabbath? Or is it a gentle tweak at the rabbi? Or a good-natured joke with his friend? With what tone does Rabbi Israel announce, "Sabbath"? Is Rabbi Israel being playful in denying the outcome of the story to Rabbi Moshe? Or is it a punishment? Or is there some deeper meaning to the denial, some lesson that the rabbi means to convey to his colleague?

The more we consider the liturgical and faith traditions behind the story, the richer and larger it becomes. Could it be that the Dantean image of the man lost in the dark woods, searching for a refuge in which to celebrate the sabbath, might be affected by those traditions? Is the irony of a fierce robber inhabiting a sanctuary heightened by those traditions? Is the fact that the story comes near its climax amid smoke significant? Or that it is told by way of a greeting? And are any of these questions means by which Rabbi Moshe, or we readers, may be able to come at the central claims of the story?

In particular, since this is a story about spiritual matters, how is Rabbi Moshe expected to be affected, even changed by this story? And how might we as readers, for whom this story has been preserved, respond in personal ways, even if we might not be part of this faith tradition, particularly as it is practiced in the early nineteenth century?

In short, how might a reader come to the spiritual center of this Hasidic tale?

I think I first became aware—I mean, truly aware—that literature provokes spiritual responses (though I would not have used that term then) in E. M. Forster's short story, "The Celestial Omnibus," introduced to me by my eighth-grade English teacher, Mr. Shamsky, a gentle Irish Catholic who loved provoking his students. In Forster's story, a young English kiddo begins to feel a transcendence inspired by beauty as he looks down Buckingham Park Road toward the poorer houses, upon which the light of sunset has its hand. "It was this cutting that had first stirred desires within the boy—desires for something just a little different, he knew not what, desires that would return whenever things were sunlit, as they were this evening, running up and down inside him, up and down, up and down, till he would feel quite unusual all over, and as likely as not would want to cry."[2]

That response leads him to poetry—which his parents and the obnoxious Mr. Bons (note the reverse spelling) force him to memorize as punishment—and the boy is astonished to read a line that seems to be describing him: "one who sits ashore and longs perchance/To visit dolphin-coral in deep seas." He suddenly realizes that poetry is speaking truth, and that realization leads him to the celestial omnibus, driven first by Sir Thomas Browne, which leads him to Tom Jones and Homer and Dickens and Wagner and John Webster and to the great Achilles and to Dante himself, whom Mr. Bons has bound in vellum but whom the boy has truly experienced. In the climax of the story—which E. M. Forster does indeed provide—Dante paraphrases the Scriptures for the boy: "Poetry is a spirit; and they that would worship it must worship in spirit and in truth." Though the boy may not understand the language, he understands the principle; he is *living* the principle.

Reading this story, I was entranced by a language that seemed to articulate what I had only vaguely intimated, a language that so strongly linked together the voice of God and the voice of poetry. I thought it was audacious, and perhaps vaguely heretical—but I also thought it was somehow true—and I wanted to understand how it could be true. I was a high school freshman, and that afternoon, after Mr. Shamsky had introduced the story to me, I walked over to Cherry Hill Books, stood at the counter, and special-ordered my first book: *The Collected Tales of E. M. Forster*. When I collected it a week later, I wrote my name in it—the first book in which I had ever done this. Then I copied the Keats sonnet onto the flyleaf. A half-century later, that volume sits beside me as I write this, sort of cocked and musty and dirtied and the jacket beat up—but still the same volume.

The book you are holding powerfully asserts that many, many books for young readers do develop characters whose lives expand with spiritual awareness and growth. Those characters learn, like Percival, to be open to transcendence, to ask questions of transcendence, and in doing so, they are affected by the answers that are revealed, or which they uncover, or which are uncovered on their behalf. Those searches provide opportunities for growth and change in those characters as they experience awe, perhaps. Or anger. Or deep confusion and puzzlement. Or joy. Or community. Or understanding. And so it seems natural that a study of such books that focuses on the searches and the answers and the responses to those answers, should yield a deeper and richer understanding of the novels, as well as a deeper and richer and very personal response to the novels—since all of this is hardly meaningful if it is not deepening for the reader. As more is uncovered, more is revealed.

Thus, for example, Dr. Seuss's *The Cat in the Hat*—which would seem an unlikely place to start in this arena. But watch how subtly Seuss asks a very deep question: by the end of the book, the Cat, along with Thing One and Thing Two, has created utter mayhem, to the consternation of the two children. When their mother approaches, they quickly kick the Cat out of the house, but are now faced with the chaos and the coming parental anger and disappointment. But, the Cat returns with his machine, order is reasserted, both the children and the fish are delighted, and the children sit and ponder this question: What will they tell their mother? Should they tell her the things that went on there that day? "Well, what would you do, if your mother asked you?"[3] And the obvious answer to this is, you would lie your head off. And perhaps you would lie like this because you don't want your mother to know that the house was just about destroyed. But more likely you would lie like this for the same reason you answered "Nothing" much of your childhood when asked what you'd been doing that day: deep down, there is a spiritual center in all of us that is utterly private and unknowable to any other mortal. Perhaps the greatest saints are able to be completely vulnerable to one another, and perhaps poets—if Thornton Wilder is correct. But otherwise, few.

When Dr. Seuss asks that question, he is asking a spiritual question. When Holden Caulfield yearns to be that catcher in the rye, he is yearning for a spiritual purpose. When Jess extends a bridge into Terabithia for MayBelle, he is extending a spiritual gift. When Dicey's grandmother allows the four children to stay with her—"Let's go home"—she is exercising a spiritual gift that she had been developing during the end of the novel. When Brian develops a connection to the rhythms and sounds and feelings of the natural world, he is moving past a dependence upon his hatchet and toward a spiritual connection with the created order that he had never before imagined. When Jacqueline Woodson's Tyrée gives up college to keep the sons of Miracle together, his act of grace is a spiritual act. When Ernesto Cisneros's Efrén overcomes his fear of defying the government and crossing the southern border to find his mother, he is asserting a spiritual value. When Jason Reynold's Will meets the ghosts of victims of gun violence on his way down in the elevator, the question he is posed is a spiritual one.

Any reading of any of these novels is incomplete without an understanding that the questions being posed, the drive of the narrative action, the purpose of the book's dramatic question, perhaps even the center of the book's meaning—these are all spiritual in nature. To not acknowledge that feels like the reader has, at the very least, missed an opportunity.

The authors of this book take this quality and concretize it in a vivid way: What if a novel was to be considered and read as a prayer? Immediately one thinks of prayer as yearning, as most books for young readers look at characters who want or need something, and who are eager and perhaps desperate to find it. And so often, what they really want—what they really really want deep down—is ever so much more than what they understand or articulate.

While sitting in the heart of Jesus, Augustus and Hazel Grace don't just want a cure for their cancers; they want an immortal love beyond boundaries, but John Green asks the reader to come to that awareness, not his characters. What Steve Harmon wants in *Monster* is not just a Not Guilty verdict; he desperately wants to be seen as he really is—but he only begins to be able to articulate that in the final line of the novel. These essays ask us to imagine these deepest yearnings as prayers, and then pose this question: What do we come to learn about the way the novels do what they do and ask what they ask when we look at them from that angle?

And so, to the second story.

Once, Rabbi Israel of Rizhyn was asked to expound on these verses from Exodus 20, 24–25: "An altar of earth thou shalt make unto me . . . and if thou wilt make me an altar of stone, thou shalt not build it of hewn stone: for it thou lift up thy tool upon it, thou hast polluted it." The rabbi answered this way: "The altar of earth is the altar of silence which is most pleasing to God. But if you do make an altar of words, do not hew and chisel them, for such artifice would profane it."

Perhaps the rabbi is suggesting that the best approach to God lies in silence. God, after all, does not need our words. But we need them. And readers of children's books, and young adult books—all of us—we need words to speak truly to those questions and about those searches that come out of our deepest selves. Artifice means nothing; authenticity means everything.

And isn't that authenticity exactly what even young children—and certainly teens—are already very, very good at discerning?

And don't all readers yearn for the authenticity of unhewn stones?

—Gary D. Schmidt, Calvin University, Grand Rapids, Michigan

Gary Schmidt is a two-time Newbery award-winning, bestselling author. His books have also won a Printz Honor and have been shortlisted for the National Book Award. He writes picture books, middle grade books, and young adult novels as well. He is also an amazing teacher. The authors recommend you read Orbiting Jupiter, Okay for Now, The Wednesday Wars, *and/or* Just Like That *as soon as you possibly can.*

NOTES

1. The two stories of Rabbi Israel of Rizhyn are here both slightly paraphrased and quoted from Martin Buber, *Tales of the Hasidim: The Later Masters.* New York: Farrar, Straus & Young, 1948. Translated by Olga Marx. 52, 59.

2. E. M. Forster, *The Collected Tales of E. M. Forster*. New York: Alfred A. Knopf, 1928, 1971. 51.

3. Dr. Seuss, *The Cat in the Hat*. New York: Random House, 1957.

Preface

This sort of thing happens all the time. We were at a conference. After Bill finished a presentation, Deb stopped to make a connection. From that, connection and a conversation grew. We were both researchers who were interested in young adult novels and were curious as to whether any research had been done on how spirituality, faith, and religion are depicted in young adult literature. Deb suggested that we should welcome Kris into the conversation, and Kris in turn suggested that her graduate assistant, Xu, would be a helpful additional voice.

We got a grant, did some research, and found that there was a lot of research on this topic, but much of that research focused on the trappings of faith, spirituality, and religion. Such studies looked for the presence of pastors, priests, shamans, rabbis, imams, and other spiritual leaders. We looked at mentions of church services, church doctrine, characters praying, and signs of spiritual commitment like baptism, confirmation, bar and bat mitzvahs, coming of age ceremonies, and so on. This was all interesting to us, but it seemed limited in its focus.

What about spiritual growth that happens outside of church, temple, mass, or mosque? What about faith mentors who are not official leaders of the church? What about main characters who grow in their faith on their own?

We first explored and experimented with a framework to chart how protagonists in young adult novels experienced spiritual or religious growth or awareness. From there we looked more widely into how protagonists grew in their relationships from a self-focused attitude to one focused on others and how protagonists became aware of something transcendent that they could connect with and that offered comfort, peace, or guidance in terms of decision-making (moral, ethical, and relationship-based).

As we did that work, however, reading young adult literature that we thought were exemplars for the sort of changes we were interested in, we kept noticing that it was rarely one single protagonist growing independently. Rather, spiritual and faith-based themes tended to permeate the entire context of the young adult novel, everything from settings to characters, from themes to point of view.

Our explorations continued. Rather than focusing only on the experiences of protagonists with faith or religion, we expanded our scope to include how such literature, when viewed in terms of a wider context, might open up moral and ethical questions, provide opportunities for characters to change and grow, and do so in a way that is deeply engaging for student readers and adult readers alike.

During this time, Bill discovered Josh Larsen's book *Movies Are Prayers: How Films Voice Our Deepest Longings*. Larsen, a former film critic with the *Naperville Sun* and current co-host of the National Public Radio program *Filmspotting* and its podcast, was considering the same questions we were, only for film. Larsen argued that audiences could consider the way movie directors engage audiences with films as a series of different types of prayers. This takes a step back from the theologically systematic, didactic, or pedagogical quantitative approaches and instead makes room for a broader interpretive range of the whole story. When the young adult novel is considered as a whole, we can see how it might function as a kind of prayer—a crying out, a pleading, a joyful shout, or a deep apology—sent from the author (and the reader) out to the larger universe.

Larsen broadly defines prayers as "guttural, personal expressions." When Larsen talks of prayers, he is not referring to the rote prayers one memorizes as a child, nor public prayers that can be performance, nor a Santa Claus letter-list of material wants. He writes:

> The prayers I knew first and still know best are guttural. They're wonderings and wanderings prompted by those moments, both sublime and sorrowful, that can't be explained by biological function of natural selection. They're instinctive recognitions of good (of things worthy of praise) and evil (of things inexplicably bent and broken.). Whenever I sense something beyond this temporal world—whether the movement of God or the machinations of wickedness—I respond, without formation or premeditation, in awe, anger, or confusion. (2017, p. 6)

In his framework, Larsen identifies several different types of prayers, including praise, yearning, lament, anger, confession, reconciliation, obedience, contemplation, and joy. Larsen is quick to point out that he is not arguing that the film writers or directors intended for their films to be viewed as prayers. Rather, Larsen views the movies he considers in his book as being "unconscious prayers."

Larsen's understanding of prayer resonated deeply with us. While he uses it to think about film, this approach also works well with young adult literature.

When we consider the analogy or prayer to talk about young adult literature, we have more language and conceptual understanding to explore what stories carry and convey.

Unfortunately, this approach brought about a problem when applied to classroom discussion. When we work with middle school, high school, and college students, we find that although they can identify overarching themes that might allow them to see *The Hate U Give* as a prayer of anger, or *Internment* as a prayer of lament, it is difficult for students to ground those discussions in the text. Class discussions instead get lost in abstractions and symbolism.

It was at that point that we stumbled upon the podcast "Harry Potter and the Sacred Text" in which two Harvard Divinity School graduates, Vanessa Zoltan and Casper ter Kuile, used techniques that have been used by rabbis, scholars, priests, imams, and pastors looking at sacred texts for well over two thousand years. Though there were many variations of these approaches, the one commonality was the idea of grounding a discussion in a small passage from the book (ranging from a sentence or two to a paragraph or two).

The scholars found that in looking at a smaller part of a sacred text, one could often see the echoes or seeds of much larger themes and ideas that ran through the whole book. Once the smaller text had been selected, it was easy to draw connections both to other texts from the same book, or to issues occurring in the society and political realities in which they were living

What Zoltan and ter Kuile did was apply those techniques to a discussion of the Harry Potter books. The huge following their podcast has is an indication of the effectiveness of this approach.

Our research group then, the four authors of this book, wondered if it would be possible to combine the overall critical perspective of Larsen's work—looking for ways in which the whole young adult book might be a specific sort of prayer when viewed as a whole, and at the same time, using sacred text techniques to keep that conversation grounded in the text,

And so we selected a wide variety of contemporary young adult texts, drawn from a range of authors, genres, and styles, then conducted both critical analyses of these texts using Larsen's approach, and piloted them in discussion with students using the sacred text approaches that Zoltan and ter Kuile called to our attention.

And that resulted in the book you now hold in your hand. It is our hope that this book will lead to fuller and more grounded discussions in general, but also more particularly to discussions about faith, spirituality, religion, and moral choices.

Acknowledgments

A book like this might look like a coming together of four scholars collaborating on an idea. In fact, however, it is a coming together of four communities of support. We have many colleagues, family members, and students whom we are thankful for.

We would all like to thank Gary Schmidt, author of a great number of excellent young adult books, each one somehow better than the last, for his support and especially for his willingness to write the forward to this volume.

Xu Bian is thankful for the opportunity to co-author this book with Drs. Boerman-Cornell, Van Duinen, and Gritter. Their knowledge, research approaches, humor, and wisdom have inspired her through the collaboration and have impacted her scholarship. She is deeply indebted to the amazing research group.

Kris Gritter would like to acknowledge a deep debt to her parents, Louis and Etta Mensonides, and is thankful for their refusal to allow a television in their home when their four children, Joel, Daniel, Eimi, and Kris, were growing up (they later rescinded that rule and Kris watched hours of television daily for years afterwards). Kris is also grateful for the way their family memorized lots of sacred texts in their home and those sparklets still come to her mind and have blessed her life. Kris is particularly grateful for Psalms 16, verse 6: "The lines are fallen unto me in pleasant places. Yea, I have a goodly heritage."

Deborah Van Duinen is grateful for the love and support of her husband Jon and her wonderfully delightful children—Claire, David, Jacob, and Eli. Reading and talking about stories as a family, in book clubs, at bedtime, on long car rides, and over cups of tea has been so life-giving over the years and continues to nourish her reading life and her love for good stories. She wishes to thank the Christian Scholars Foundation and InterVarsity's Emerging Scholars Network for their grant which supported our group's early work on this topic.

Bill Boerman-Cornell would like to thank Deb, Kris, and Xu for researching, writing, and laughing together (Go Lady Scholars Plus Bill!) in friendship and collaboration. He would also like to thank Trinity Christian College for granting him a Summer Research Grant in 2021 which allowed him to spend time with his co-authors finishing up the final chapters of the book, and Chicago Semester for the Scholars-in-Residence Fellowship, which gave him time to proofread and index this book.

Thanks to our editor Carlie Wall for her support and help. Thanks too to the entire team at Rowman & Littlefield from assistant editors to layout designers, proofreaders, and publicity and promotions folks.

Thanks too to the graduate students in Bill's Education 562 class—Kristin Bolkema, Hannah Meyrick, Britta Slager, and Brandi Smits—for piloting the techniques used in this book. Bill would also like to thank his friends Rick and John for their support, his brothers Tom and Mike, his parents, and most importantly, his children—Kathryn, Frances. and Will—and his amazing wife Amy who is a better teacher than he will ever be. Their patience while he hunched over his Surface tablet, writing one more sentence as everyone waited to leave on an outing or vacation, is something he is deeply grateful for.

Chapter 1

Prayers of Lament in *Internment*

In Samira Ahmed's young adult novel *Internment*, a dystopian novel set in a near-future United States, high school student Layla Amin and her family are relocated to an interment camp merely because they are Muslim. The military-run camp, which is reminiscent of Japanese American internment camps during World War II, severely restricts even the basic constitutional freedoms of the American citizens who are relocated there. Layla finds her voice in the camp and finds ways to share with the world the oppression and betrayal of democratic ideals that are occurring in the camp. In short, *Internment* is a young adult text which functions as Ahmed's prayer of lament. *Internment*, published in 2019, was a *New York Times* Bestseller and was nominated for an Abe Lincoln Award and a Keystone to Reading Award. We selected this book on the strength of the authorial voice and the connections it makes to a young adult audience. Ahmed's other young adult novels include *Love, Hate, and Other Filters* (2018); and *Mad, Bad, and Dangerous to Know* (2020).

One way to see *Internment* is as a prayer of lament. Josh Larsen defines lament in this way: "Yet at its fullest, biblical lament expresses sorrow over losing a world that was once good alongside a belief that it can be made good again" (2017, p. 51). *Internment* is set in a very near future where, with just a small nudge, distrust and hatred for Muslims results in action—the government reopens internment camps and strips away its citizens' freedom on the basis of the religion they believe in or the culture they are a part of. The main character, Layla, laments the loss of the world she had as much as the reality of the new, horrible world she is now experiencing.

In this chapter we describe how the sacred text reading practice of florilegium can be a way to discover how the text develops the theme of lament throughout the story. In the years we have taught *Internment* to our undergraduate students, students have responded emotionally and personally to this powerful text.

FULLER SUMMARY OF *INTERNMENT*

In *Internment,* readers are introduced to high school student Layla Amin who has been living a comfortable life as the daughter of professionals (her father is a highly regarded writer whose poems are included in the novel and her mother is a chiropractor). Amin is a well-read student, an observant Muslim, and is experiencing first love with David, her Jewish boyfriend.

A new president of the United States is elected who incites distrust and hatred toward Muslims, then suggests establishing internment camps for Muslim Americans. Some of the nameless president's quotes will be reminiscent of, if not verbatim, quotes from a particular recent presidential administration. Ahmed structures the novel as a prayer of lament easily recognized by young adult literature readers once they have the vocabulary and conceptual knowledge to see it.

At the beginning of the book, Layla is already living in fear. The president has decreed that Muslims must register their religious status. Her parents have lost their jobs. The national legislature has passed exclusion laws. The family is not living in hiding, but they recognize patterns in the direction of societal trends that are reminiscent of life in Germany preceding the Holocaust of World War II. They have little recourse or agency and can do little but lament their situation and hope things will not get worse.

Soon the family is relocated to Mobius, an internment camp. In fact, Mobius is at the very site of Manzanar, the desert camp where Japanese Americans were incarcerated during World War II. The camp is surrounded by electric fences and heavily monitored by cameras. Muslims are separated by ethnicity and culture, which is meant to stifle collective action from the beginning and encourage distrust and infighting. With each new crackdown, each new rule, and each new oppression by the camp commander, Layla's world looks less like how the reader perceives America ought to look, and at the same time, there is more to grieve.

Layla notices one guard, Jake, is different than the other guards. In fact, he is working for a rebellion for social justice, which is unknown to the other authorities of the camp.

Layla has courage, language skill, and an abundance of strategic plans, largely because of her wide reading and knowledge of her religion. Furtively, she forms connections with Muslims inside the camp outside of her immediate culture, noting who are likely to be people of action. She also mobilizes Jake, who allows her to be in contact with David. Much of the rebellion occurs because of the tools of technology and social media. But even as it occurs, Layla is forced again and again to make choices that may endanger her family, put her fellow prisoners at risk, or threaten her own safety and even her life. Her frustration, anxiety, and despair continues to build.

Eventually, the inmates are released (as young adult literature traditionally ends with hope or casts a vision of eventual hope, even in dystopian fiction), but not without violence and heartbreaking loss. As we noted, the college students who read this book as part of the Young Adult Literature classes we teach find this to be a powerful read and many have said the book brought them to tears.

INTERNMENT AS A PRAYER OF LAMENT

Theological scholar Nancy Lee notes that a lament is "an ancient human phenomenon of expression with a long and wide-ranging history as well as an ever-present reality" (2010). Lament starts as an oral utterance that is written down with a specific format that gives structure to the writer who wishes to emphasize their sorrow or distress, or document it.

Lee notes that in sacred texts there are two main genres of lament: "Lament as prayerful plea to God for help and/or a complaint to God over social injustice" and "lament as a dirge about the death or destruction of something or someone" (2010, p. 1). The first kind of lament is more common in the Bible, especially the Psalms and Lamentations. The second kind is more common in literature and even songs of popular culture. Lee mentions Elton John and Bernie Taupin's song "Candle in the Wind," a dirge composed for Marilyn Monroe in its first iteration and Princess Diana in a reiteration of the song years later.

Besides lamenting the death of one we love, a dirge can also include a lament over the death of creation by lack of creation care. Not only a Judeo-Christian literacy practice, laments also show up in ancient Mesopotamian cultures and other civilizations showing signs of distress. The Qur'an, Lee notes, includes laments as when Abraham prays, "Praise be to Allah, Who hath granted unto me an old age Isma'il and Isaac: for truly my Lord is He, the Hearer of Prayer" (Sura 14:39, cited in Lee, 2010, p. 4). Lee also cites a lament by Lakota elder, John Hallow Horn, who observes the earth laments because of bad care of the land and greedy human choices leading to eventual death (p. 7).

In seeing *Internment* as a prayer of lament, we draw on Lee's description of the seven parts of the kind of lament that is typical in the Psalms. This framework allows us to see the ways in which *Internment* functions as a prayer of lament which Samira Ahmed is getting at with the novel. While the novel doesn't necessarily follow the structure of a prayer of lament in order, all the components are there.

Lee begins by first suggesting that prayers of lament initially address the deity (often in second-person speech). Early on in *Internment,* soldiers come to Layla's home to take her family into custody and deliver them to the internment camp. The arrival of the soldiers is sudden, and the family is given only ten minutes to pack up whatever they want to bring with them. Before Layla can text her boyfriend David, the soldiers take her cell phone.

In that moment of shock, anger, and despair, Layla remembers how her Nanni carried a laminated card of the Verse of the Throne, a protection prayer from the Quran. She recalls the middle line: "He knows that which is in front of them and that which is behind them" (p. 37). Although this is not second-person speech, Layla references a protecting deity. This practice of her Nanni is not only a fond memory for Layla, but also a comfort in the trauma of being taken from their home.

The second part of the form that prayers of lament follow is to articulate a complaint or description of distress, often with questions (to or against the deity, about one's enemies, or about one's suffering). At the end of the same chapter mentioned in the previous paragraph, Layla and her family have been taken from their home in front of their neighbors and put into the back of a police car. As the car pulls away, Layla sees someone running toward them. She wonders if it is David, but because of the interior light in the car, she can only see her own reflection and is struck by how much the image does not look like her.

Layla has lost her home, her freedoms, and even her identity as a Muslim American. Her world has fragmented and all she has left is other people whose worlds have been similarly shattered. While Layla's cry doesn't specifically address a diety, her voice is clearly a crying out. Since the book is written in first-person point of view from Layla's perspective, this voicing of narration isn't unusual, but this particular quote has the quality of a lament being directed to a deity.

The third step is to express trust in the deity and/or remembrance of past saving actions. While this idea comes up in multiple parts of the book, perhaps Layla's mother articulates it best after Soheil, Layla's friend from the camp, rushes the perimeter fence during a protest and is electrocuted to death. Layla feels like she is trapped in a nightmare. She is sick and cannot even stand after witnessing Soheil's death. She runs to her mom who embraces her and tells her it is okay. Layla responds that it is not okay and that she doubts that anything will ever be okay again. Then Layla tells her mother what happened.

Her mother goes pale, she cries, and then gathers herself and seems to find comfort in her faith in her deity. After a pause, she tells Layla that they belong to Allah and shall go back to him one day. Then Layla's mother prays that Allah would be merciful to Soheil and welcome him into heaven (p. 300).

When we think of a YA book as a prayer, it is important to remember that the author does not speak only through a single protagonist. The theme or subject of the prayer the author is writing is woven through multiple characters and storylines.

The fourth aspect of a prayer of lament, according to Lee, is to create a plea or petition to the deity. This plea might include imperative verbs and might ask for vengeance or a righting of wrongs. After Jake the guard arranges a meeting between Layla and David; and after David, in desperation and fear for her safety, suggests that Layla turn informer for the government; when it feels like Layla has lost all hope, Jake whispers the phrase *insha'Allah* (p. 159).

When Jake says this, he is creating a plea. According to Mary McMahon (2021), "The phrase insha'Allah means 'God willing' or 'if God wills it' in Arabic." Devout Muslims say "insha'Allah" whenever they make a statement about a plan to do something, as away of requesting God's blessing on that activity. The phrase also acknowledges submission to God, with the speaker putting him or herself into God's hands and accepting the fact that God sometimes works in inscrutable ways.

Lee notes that in some prayers of lament, this is the point where a transition might occur to indicate that the person making the plea received aid. While there are moments of something like hope in *Internment*, such moments are often crushed soon after.

Lee describes three final stages in a prayer of lament. The person praying conveys the utter assurance of being heard, they offer a vow of praise, and they praise the deity. In *Internment*, this moment doesn't come until the very end of the book. In those last sentences, Layla speaks of being delivered from her oppression. While she says that she is unclear about exactly what her next steps will be, she believes she will figure it out. She will move forward and will not look back (p. 373). While there is not obvious recognition of a deity here, and certainly no praise or promise of praise for that deity, it is not difficult to conclude that the author's prayer of lament has been heard and change has come.

One aspect of dystopian fiction is that it imagines a world even more broken than the one we live in. Samir Ahmed sets this world up so that it can be a focus for the lament she feels about the hatred and xenophobia that are so present in our post–9/11 world. But she also makes it a world where those prayers of lament are heard, and change (or at least limited deliverance) has come.

If studying *Internment* with students, it may be helpful to see the form that a prayer of lament takes in a sacred text. An example of this form can be seen in the Old Testament book of Habakkuk, chapter 3. We have labeled the parts of the form according to Lee's structure. Lines have been removed from this excerpt in order to concentrate on the structure.

A Prayer of Habakkuk the Prophet

Addressing the deity (second-person speech)
Lord, I have heard of your fame;
I stand in awe of your deeds, Lord.
Repeat them in our day,
in our time make them known;
in wrath remember mercy. . . .

Articulate description of distress
Plague went before him;
pestilence followed his steps.
He stood, and shook the earth;
he looked, and made the nations tremble. . . .

Trust in the deity/remembrance of past saving actions
You came out to deliver your people,
to save your anointed one.
You crushed the leader of the land of wickedness,
you stripped him from head to foot. . . .

Create a plea/petition to the deity
I heard and my heart pounded,
my lips quivered at the sound;
decay crept into my bones,
and my legs trembled.
Yet I will wait patiently for the day of calamity
to come on the nation invading us.
Though the fig tree does not bud
and there are no grapes on the vines,
though the olive crop fails
and the fields produce no food,
though there are no sheep in the pen
and no cattle in the stalls,

Assurance of being heard/vow of praise
yet I will rejoice in the Lord,
I will be joyful in God my Savior.
The Sovereign Lord is my strength;
he makes my feet like the feet of a deer,
he enables me to tread on the heights

USING FLORILEGIUM AS A WHOLE CLASS TO DISCUSS *INTERNMENT*

As mentioned in the introductory chapter, the podcast *Harry Potter and the Sacred Text* uses the sacred reading practice of florilegium. The podcast's hosts explain that the word *florilegium* comes from Latin and means "a collection of flowers." As they read, monks would focus on sparklets, lines of text that they found important and insightful, lines that jumped off the pages of sacred text and into their hearts. Monks would fill pages of journals with sparklets, sometimes creating texts where sparklets could be categorized by theme. They created a new text when they combined all of these excerpts from text.

This is similar to an activity Kris has been doing with her students for many years: reading a text and noting the "golden line" in that text as the line that most stood out to that reader. People who appreciate good quotes engage in florilegium as well. The practice of writing found poetry could be described as a form of florilegium. People who write down funny or interesting pieces of dialogue engage in this practice. In fact, many tweets are the beginnings of florilegium. When many sparklets are brought together, the spiritual practice of florilegium happens.

Sometimes the best discussion can begin out of a small door into the text, however, rather than a cacophony of favorite lines. Florilegium works by (1) considering the meaning and context of sparklets or golden lines separately, (2) bringing two sparklets or golden lines together, (3) considering what meaning emerges from the juxtaposition of the two lines, (4) considering what the combination of the two lines has to say about the overarching theme that the class is considering, and (5) attempting to make sense of the corpus of knowledge that has been created by extending the meaning to the lives of the participants and what they already know.

The practice of florilegium asks a community of insightful readers to collect comments and insights from texts they have read. The idea is to place selected phrases or sentences in conversation with one another. Passages then connect to other passages. Readers articulate the connections they make as individual readers and then sparklets are connected across readers.

In one of Bill's classes, he begins by asking students to each nominate a significant sentence from *Internment* that connected for them in some way to the idea of the book as a prayer of lament. Once the class has heard all of the nominations, they choose two to concentrate on:

"And your death would mean as much as any other death, sound and fury signifying nothing." (p. 329)

"What use are my words in the face of this?" (p. 94)

Bill asks the students who nominated these sentences to explain the context of each. The first student explains that the first sentence occurs toward the end of the book when Layla has been put in a holding cell and is meeting with the director of the internment camp. Layla's efforts to protest and call attention to the injustices in the camp have infuriated the director. He is threatening her and trying to minimize her efforts and he says that she has no power, and that further, her martyrdom would be old news after two days and that her death would accomplish nothing.

The second sentence comes from earlier in the book (as we will see, the initial order of the sentences matters little). It is shortly after Layla and her family arrive in the internment camp. Everyone in the camp has gathered for an orientation. As the director explains the features of the camp, and tells how each section of the camp will have "minders" who will watch over the internees (and listen in on their conversations and report to the director), a woman in the crowd accuses the minders of being traitors. The director motions to the guards and the woman resists. The guards tase her and drag her from the room. At that point Layla reflects that her words are useless in this situation (though later she will find that is not the case).

After the students who nominated the lines provide the context in which those lines appear, the teacher then reads the two lines back-to-back in the order they appear above. Bill then asks the students what they notice about the two lines. One student says that the first sentence seems to be encouraging, in a way, saying that it is not worth sacrificing oneself if that sacrifice will not make a difference. By itself, that line sounds like someone trying to talk someone else out of sacrificing their life. But then the second sentence seems to be more of a statement of futility. Even as the sacrifice of a life would be meaningless, so are words—because the lamentable situation the characters find themselves in seems to offer no way out.

Another student points out that the first sentence is suggesting that not only would the speaker's death be pointless, but further that it would be as pointless as any other death would be. The implication is that the problem isn't that this kind of sacrifice would be meaningless but because other types of death could be more meaningful. Rather, this death is as pointless as every other death is.

After these initial analyses, the class spends some time talking about the ways in which the internment camp accentuates the desperation by making not only rebellion against the oppression nearly impossible, but also making it hard for the residents of the camp to think of themselves as anything other than creatures in danger, certainly not as citizens of a republic that is based on the idea that they have rights.

After the conversation goes on for a time, Bill reverses the order of the two quotes and reads them again:

"What use are my words in the face of this?"

"And your death would mean as much as any other death, sound and fury signifying nothing."

Bill again asks students what they see in the intersection of these two sparklets.

One student immediately suggests that this arrangement seems even more hopeless. In this arrangement, words are of no use, but further, even sacrificing one's life doesn't matter. Bill asks if this pairing reminds them of any other moment from the book. This opens the door for a wide-ranging discussion that brings in many of the nominated quotes from before, and leads to a discussion of the ways that the novel is lamenting not only the situation of the characters in the book, but the overarching ways in which humans divide themselves and throw up barriers of hatred and misunderstanding in so many ways.

Throughout this conversation, the teacher should be intentional about valuing all comments and welcoming all insights. This assures students that if they make an observation, even one which they are not certain of, that observation will always be treated as a contribution, not as an irrelevant or banal comment. The teacher should make sure that no one's contribution is devalued or made fun of.

Another variant is to assign each student (or pairs of students) a chapter. They then find the single quote from that chapter that stands out the most. The teacher can then work through the book, pairing quotes from every two consecutive chapters together. When Bill has used this in his classes, he has found that while some quote pairings lead to more interesting insights than others, working through the book in this way will spur several interesting discussions at the least. It is also good, toward the end of the exercise, to remind students to be aware of the way the progression of quotes may help us see growth and change through the book.

SEEING THE SPIRITUAL PRACTICE OF FLORILEGIUM WITHIN *INTERNMENT*

Layla, the protagonist of *Internment*, is highly literate in that she is well-read and has a good understanding of popular culture. In a sense, she has collected golden lines and sparklets throughout this novel and shares them with the reader. Kris asked her students to use the quotes that Layla selected, her florilegium lines, as the sparklets to discuss. The sentences that Layla loves then become the focus of a deeper dive into her character.

What follows is a list of the important lines Layla records in her journal—lines she has read, heard, and experienced or constructed by writing or speaking with others, often alluding to what she has read, viewed, or consumed in her literacy practices. These sparklets are arranged according to the steps of lament.

LAYLA'S FLORILEGIA ACCORDING TO THE STEPS OF LAMENT

1. Addressing the deity
   - Mom's prayer on page 300 proclaiming that they belong to Allah and will return to him and asking mercy for Soheil and a welcome into heaven.
   - The communal prayer over Jake's body after he gave his life to save Layla. This prayer asks God to forgive Jake for whatever sins he has and to again welcome him into heaven (p. 368).
2. Articulate complaint or description of distress, often with questions (to or against the deity, about one's enemies, or about one's suffering)
   - The story *The White Rose*, about the siblings from World War II who wrote of their resistance to the Nazis, passes to David to spread to the media. Sophie Scholl, the sister in the story, makes the particularly important point that someone has to start change happening (p. 184).
   - The signs of the protesters outside the gates note the suffering of the incarcerated asking for freedom for those who have been interns, an end to anti-Muslim hatred, and a welcome for all (p. 229).
3. Expressing trust in the deity and/or remembrance of past saving actions
   - Verses from the Quran, especially "The Verse of the Throne," which proclaims that Allah knows both the future and the past.
   - Nanni's prayer she said in India when she was afraid of the British asking God to protect her in whatever way God wishes to (p. 227).
4. Creating a plea/petition to the deity (uses imperative verbs; may include call for vengeance)
   - The Ayat passage that Layla's parents quote says that religion should not be something that is forced and that one Muslim should not judge another Muslim's religiosity.
   - Khadijah's auntie quotes Layla's father's poetry about bearing witness, listening, and praying (p. 351).
5. Utter assurance of being heard and praise to deity

- Layla's statement that when she is feeling isolated and without hope, looking at the infinity of the night sky helps her know the eternal depth of love (p. 325).
- Layla's revelation that when one listens to one's heart's silence, then one can hear it roaring (p. 143).

USING FLORILEGIUM WITH PARTNERS TO GAIN INSIGHTS INTO *INTERNMENT*

The sparklet that stood out to Kris (from the list above) were two lines of Layla's father's poetry, "We shall bear witness/On the Night of Destiny/As a hush descends/And a prayer rises" (p. 351). Kris plucks these lines as dialogue that Khadijah's auntie offers as part of a larger quote when she notes that Layla is the heartbeat of the rebellion, offering Layla a symbol of identity. Layla responds to Khadijah's auntie that the heartbeat is the power of all voices demanding justice, observing her role comes from the needs of her people, a situation similar to that of Esther in the Bible.

Kris partners with Bill. She asks Bill what his sparklet would be from the list above. He selects, "Only when you open yourself to the heart's silence can you hear its roar." He contextualizes this quote with Layla's father's interpretation of the quote that it is meant to be a reminder that those who do not speak up are not always weak (p. 143).

They rearrange both lines and Bill reads their selected lines aloud slowly: "We shall bear witness/On a Night of Destiny/As a hush descends/And a prayer rises . . . you open yourself to the heart's silence [so you can] hear its roar."

They note how both passages reference sound, juxtaposing "hush," an absence of sound, with the word "roar," a full-bodied sound. Kris reads the lines in reverse order, "Only when you open yourself to the heart's silence can you hear its roar / As a hush descends / And a prayer rises / On a Night of Destiny / We shall bear witness." Kris asks if there is a time when they found silence to be loud, especially when they were anxious to hear about the health and well-being of themselves and loved ones in times of emergency.

Bill mentions a time when his wife was pregnant with their first daughter and the doctor was unable to find a heartbeat. In those days, more than two decades ago, the doctor recommended waiting a couple of weeks and then trying to hear the heartbeat again. While Bill and his wife waited, the world was as noisy as ever, but their hearts felt the silence. And Bill says it was the loudest silence he has ever experienced. Two weeks later, when the doctor's microphone revealed a whispered heartbeat, quiet but strong, the roaring silence was replaced by a roaring whisper—and that whispered roar is one of the best sounds Bill has ever heard in his life.

Bill and Kris connect their lines with the whole novel. Layla cannot advocate vocally for herself and her people at all times. Sometimes she has to watch and listen and take her cues from what goes on around her. Kris equates her character with the biblical character of Esther, who uses her speaking time with the king judiciously and listens to her uncle Mordecai before acting.

Layla could only act when Camp Mobius has sufficiently coalesced as a group, regardless of national and ethnic differences, to participate in their own emancipation. Layla was a prominent voice in this process, but only one voice. Social movements do not work with only one voice speaking. If someone wishes to speak for a group, they must first hear and understand the needs of the group. If they do not, they cannot speak for the group.

Because Kris and Bill are both teachers who teach this book, they talk about how they could extend this activity with the classes they teach. They would ask their students to search *Internment* looking for florilegia that reference silence or speaking up. They would ask their students to explain their selection: Why did they pick that line? Why do they love it? What does it reveal about the nature of silence? Bill and Kris would place all quotes front and center and have students reflect on what the cumulative lines reveal about speaking up for a group that is being persecuted or mistreated.

As both of these examples show, even when focusing specifically on the theme of lament, *Internment* offers a wide variety of possible passages to serve as our entrée into the text. Any of those pairings will result in a fruitful discussion that stays focused on the text and also links moments from student's lives to the moments in the book. Whether teachers chose to engage florilegium as a whole class or in partner groups, the conversations that result will be both insightful and fun.

Chapter 2

Yearning in *The Hate U Give*

Prayers of yearning can take many forms. Sometimes these prayers express our desires for what we want back. A beautiful beach scene from our childhood. A time when we were happy with family or friends. Moments in our lives when things seemed simpler or when they made more sense. Often these yearnings or longings are unfulfillable. Nostalgia for a past season, relationship, or experience is for something that has already happened. People and places inevitably change, as do we, and so these yearnings can't be fulfilled. Yet we often still have them.

Sometimes our yearning is for something in the future: a fulfilling relationship, completion of a college degree, finally starting a career, retirement, children, or grandchildren.

But sometimes our prayers of yearning express something that we can't fully articulate but that represents a desire for more of something. Listening to the final chorus in Handel's *Messiah*, for example, can make us ache for something that we can't describe.

Larsen describes yearning this way, "When we offer a yearning prayer, we're something like [the Biblical character] Nicodemus, stealing into the dark night . . . seeking illumination on the irresistible mystery that is Christ. When movies spill out from the projection booth into the theater, they're venturing into a similar darkness, and looking for the same source of light. . . . Is there something or someone beyond our earthly existence who can satisfy our souls?" (2017, p. 37).

And it isn't just film. Young adult literature can capture the intensity of yearning that goes along with the transition for childhood into adulthood. It is a yearning for identity, completeness, and most of all, clarity of calling. What are we meant to do in the world? How do we respond to the injustice around us? There must be something more to live for. There must be something different that this broken world. Whatever that something is, it feels just beyond our reach.

In various religious traditions, our yearnings for something more or different have often been described as yearnings rooted in who we are as humans and at what we were created to do and be. In a 1964 essay, J. R. R. Tolkien wrote about a final joy that lies "beyond the walls of the world." In St. Augustine's prayer at the beginning of his *Confessions*, he addresses God with these words: "You have made us for yourself, and our heart is restless until it rests in you" (1992, p. 3).

Our yearnings or longings point to a larger purpose or design for the human experience. Framed in these ways, our yearnings can show us that what is happening here and now is not the full picture. To paraphrase C. S. Lewis, our secret is that we are filled with yearnings, both shy and passionate, and those yearnings direct us to go beyond the objects of earth to seek the ultimate reality of God.

And yet, those yearnings are also rooted in the world we are in and its shortcomings. We wish for a world that is more just, a world where all people are valued fully, regardless of their economic station, religious affiliation, culture, vocation, or the color of their skin. We long for a world that is safe for everyone, not just those who can afford protection. We long for a world without poverty, war, misunderstanding, anger, hatred, disease, pain, and suffering. Becoming aware of the injustice in the world and yearning to help remake the world into something better is part of adolescence and young adulthood.

As we considered young adult books that offered prayers of yearning, we thought immediately of Angie Thomas's (2017) *The Hate U Give*. Thomas's book and its story about police brutality and systemic racism could also be studied as a prayer of lament, as these prayers are indeed embedded in this story in powerful ways.

But as we read and studied Thomas's debut novel, we decided to highlight this book as offering a glimpse into what prayers of yearning can look like. Swirling in and around prayers of lament in *The Hate U Give* are also prayers of yearning for what could and should be in our broken world. Starr Carter's story offers readers prayers of yearning for light in the darkness, a phrase taken from the book's dedication page. *The Hate U Give* is a story of lament, yearning, and hope.

The Hate U Give had its beginnings in 2009. Thomas first wrote the story during her senior year in college in reaction to the police shooting of Oscar Grant. Years later, she turned it into a novel that also became a successful film. *The Hate U Give* debuted at number one on the *New York Times* young adult best-seller list and stayed on that list for 236 weeks as of October of 2021. In 2018, it was the winner of the William C. Morris award for best debut book for teens, the Coretta Scott King award for best novel by an

African American author for children, and an honor book for the Michael Prinz Award for the best novel for teens.

Thomas has two other books that connect to the characters in *The Hate U Give*: *On the Come Up* (2019), and *Concrete Rose*.

In *The Hate U Give,* Starr Carter is a 16-year-old black girl who lives in the mostly poor black neighborhood of Garden Heights but attends a predominantly white private school, Williamson Prep. Starr straddles the two vastly different worlds and navigates their differences by keeping them distinct and separate. She reflects on her experience at school, thinking about how, as one of the only black kids at the school, she is cool almost automatically (p. 15). But being cool is only part of the story. Starr also morphs into "Starr version two" at school and code-switches so that she fits in. She describes two versions of herself. Williamson Starr, the version of herself at school, avoids slang, even if her white friends use it because it makes them cool and makes her seem like she is from the 'hood. Williamson Starr keeps her emotions bottled up when someone makes her angry. She is nice. Normal Starr is allowed free rein of her emotions and can act how she likes when she is at home (p. 71).

Starr's two best friends at Williamson, Hailey Grant and Maya Young, and her white boyfriend, Chris, don't have any idea of who Starr is in her Garden Heights world. In Garden Heights, Starr is a responsible daughter who gets good grades, helps around the house, and is a supportive sister to her brothers and a loyal friend to Kenya and the other kids she grew up in her Garden Heights neighborhood.

Part 1 of the book begins with Starr at a weekend party with her friends from Garden Heights. A shooting breaks up the party and Starr's childhood best friend, Khalil, offers to drive her home. On the way they are stopped by a white police officer who orders Khalil to exit the car. While standing outside the car, Khalil leans into the driver-side window to check in on Starr. Thinking that Khalil is reaching for a gun, the officer fires three shots and kills Khalil.

Part 2 of the book takes place five weeks after Khalil's death. Part 3 is 8 weeks after, Part 4 is 10 weeks after and Part 5 is 13 weeks after the death of Khalil. In Part 5, the jury decides whether to indict the white police officer for the death of Khalil.

In the climax of the novel, Starr and her friends successfully defend the store that belongs to Starr's father, Maverick, from King, a gang leader. The whole neighborhood stands up to King and as a result of testimony from DeVante, King is arrested and expected to be in jail for a long time. The book ends with Starr promising to keep Khalil's memory alive and continue her fight against injustice.

YEARNING FOR JUSTICE

The book's title references a Tupac Shakur quote describing life as a Black man. At the beginning of the story, right before he is murdered, Khalil explains this quote to Starr. He says that Thug Life, according to Shakur, is an acronym describing how the injustice society gives Black youth results in everybody suffering (p. 17).

Starr thinks about her two worlds and how the violence she sometimes sees or hears about in Garden Heights is part of a larger societal structure. Later in the story, Starr and her dad, Maverick, also talk about Thug Life. Starr says that although Khalil believed that what society does to Black children comes back to hurt all of society later, Starr herself believes that it is about all Black people, and even more broadly, all people who are politically, economically, or in any other way marginalized.

Starr's dad, Maverick, explains and encourages Starr to think about how this theory goes way back even further than the Panthers. Starr sees the truth in this and concludes that Khalil got tired of having to chose between eating and keeping the lights on (p. 169) and that's why he became a drug dealer. She later reflects on how DeVante and Khalil found themselves in impossible situations and she says that she isn't sure that, if their places were switched, she would have decided any better than they did (p. 239).

Starr yearns for a world in which Khalil's life matters. She yearns for there to be justice for his death and for his memory to focus on his life. She yearns for a time when black people don't need to have "the talk" that she received from her father about how, if she is pulled over, Starr should keep her hands where they can be seen, not move suddenly, and only talk to the officer if the officer talks to her (p. 22).

YEARNING FOR A VOICE

The only witness to Khalil's shooting is Starr, and she needs to decide what to say or do, if anything, since her identity as the key witness is initially kept secret. Starr's mom wants to protect her from public scrutiny as Khalil's death quickly becomes national news, and Starr herself isn't sure if she wants to speak out. The media portrays Khalil as a drug dealer and gang member and describes the white police officer in more favorable terms.

Starr also knows that when young people of color speak out, they can be unfairly criticized. When Rachel Jeantel testified against her friend, Trayvon Martin's killer George Zimmerman, she was heavily criticized for the language she used and for what some people perceived as holes in her story.

As the story moves ahead, something changes in Starr. She decides that she wants to speak out for her friend who was unable to defend himself, his complicated life choices, and the events that happened that night. It is clear that Starr not only yearns for things to have been different in the past, but she also yearns for the world to be a place of justice and safety where all people are fully valued. Starr remembers seeing her other best friend, Natasha, die at age ten after a gang member opened fire on her block. At the time, Starr didn't talk about it or let people know that she identified the shooter.

We learn later that Starr witnessed the murder and could identify the tattooed shooter. She remained silent to protect herself and was proud that she didn't snitch. For years, Starr held the secret of knowing who killed Natasha and the shame of not being brave enough to tell someone.

Starr ends up deciding to use her voice, her weapon, to change the narrative about Khalil and to speak out against the injustice around her. She doesn't agree with how the media portrays Khaili and wants to help others see the implications of poverty, hunger, and the need to care for one's family. A combination of anger and yearning for things to be different leads her to agree to be the star witness in the grand jury trial.

When the grand jury fails to indict the white officer, there are peaceful protests and riots in Garden Heights. Starr realizes that she also needs to participate in the protests that follow the decision. She takes an increasingly public role—giving a television interview and then speaking out during the protests, finding the courage to respond to the trauma of seeing Khalil's death and to do so politically. Starr seeks to change an entrenched system of power.

YEARNING FOR MEANING

At Khalil's funeral, Starr wrestles with making sense of his death. The choir sings upbeat songs and almost everybody claps and joins in praising Jesus. Starr's mom sings along and waves her hands. Khalil's grandma and auntie clap and sing too. People run around the sanctuary dancing, their feet moving like James Brown and their bent arms flapping like chicken wings (p. 127).

Starr, however, can't join in. She reasons that if Khalil is not celebrating, she can't either. She doesn't know how she can praise a God that let Khalil get shot. In that context, the funeral doesn't make any sense to her (p. 127).

As the book progresses, Starr continues to yearn for meaning in what is happening around her. She looks at the stick-on glow-in-the-dark stars on her bedroom ceiling and thinks about her father telling her that he named her Starr because she was like light in the darkness for him. She thinks about how she needs light in her own darkness (p. 256).

Later, Starr's mom relates the story of Starr's birth. Her mom tells her that when she was born, she wasn't able to breathe on her own at first. Her mom recalls that she started to panic and Maverick couldn't calm her down. He was freaked out himself. And then, after a long moment, baby Starr let out a cry. Her mom was convinced that she had done something wrong. A nurse told her that even though things can go wrong no matter how hard one tries to make them go right, one has to keep going (p. 154).

While that advice doesn't necessarily solve everything, it does point to what one can do in response to a yearning to find meaning.

YEARNING FOR A COHESIVE SENSE OF SELF

Starr also yearns for an integrated sense of who she is. Coinciding with Starr's yearning for justice, meaning, and a voice, is her realization that straddling both of her worlds is increasingly difficult and not something she wants, or is able, to keep doing. The carefully built-up boundary between Starr's two worlds begins to crumble when she is overwhelmed by the pressure of testifying before a grand jury and the responsibility of speaking out in Khalil's memory. She can't keep up her constructed identity of Starr 2.0. In a critical scene, she confronts Hailey who insists that Khalil was a criminal. Since part of being Starr 2.0 was avoiding conflict, especially about race, she feels her separate identities melting together.

By exploring Starr's motivations, fears, hopes, and regrets, Thomas shows us a character who is fully human. In many ways, readers see Starr in ways that Starr doesn't yet see herself. We see her on her own terms and not the stereotypical versions of her seen by others. As readers, we envision new possibilities for black girls like Starr, but also new visions of our collective humanity.

In part 4 of the story, Starr's two worlds begin to overlap in ways they haven't before. Chris, Maya, and Kenya and DeVante all meet. Starr reflects that her two different worlds crashed into each other, but to her astonishment, everything turned out okay (p. 359).

Starr realizes that in order to be true to herself and her community, she needs to live into her identity as someone from Garden Heights. Her friend Kenya points out that Starr seems ashamed of Kenya, Khalil, and her whole neighborhood. After some reflection, Starr realizes that Kenya is right. She has been ashamed of the Garden and all that it contains. After thinking about it she realizes that she can't change where she came from and her experiences, and it was foolish to think she should hide them. There is no sense, she thinks, in being ashamed of what she is. Starr decides she will not live that way any more (p. 441).

Starr yearns to be able to be herself instead of having to morph into different versions of herself depending on her racial and economic context, and the reader sees her begin that journey.

YEARNING FOR HOPE

We can see *The Hate U Give* as a prayer of yearning, not just for Starr but also for readers of the story because of the way Thomas uses Starr's first-person account to build empathy in her readers. Her readers have different degrees to which they have been affected by events like those described in the book. Some readers can take comfort in recognizing in Starr someone else who has faced similar challenges including needing to code-switch between school and home. Other readers are further removed from any direct experience with protests or having injustice touch someone they know; Starr's experience can help give them deeper understanding and empathy.

In seeing the story and its events from Starr's perspective, Thomas invites in readers who might not otherwise have picked up a book about Black Lives Matter or systematic racism. The story shows the weight of bearing witness.

Thomas, however, encourages her readers to go beyond just empathy. We can join Starr in yearning for a better world, a better understanding of our collective humanity. We can yearn for more and work toward what the world could be by including realism in the story—naming real-world victims of police brutality such as Tamir Rice and Michael Brown.

In placing Starr's struggles in this larger historical context, Thomas encourages her readers to act, to join her and Starr in their yearning for and commitment to finding and working toward the light in the darkness. She gives us a better understanding of entrenched prejudice—where it comes from and what role Starr and readers have in exposing and combating it.

LECTIO DIVINA AND *THE HATE U GIVE*

There are many ways to discuss this book as a prayer of yearning with students, but we want to suggest Lectio Divina as one possibility.

Lectio Divina is Latin for "sacred reading" and is a contemplative practice with Christian roots in the Benedictine tradition. It is used to refer to an approach wherein you pick or choose a given sentence, phrase, or word through which God speaks. Traditionally, this is done with scripture. It draws on the way Jewish people read the Haggadah, a text read during Passover that retells the Exodus story. *Haggadah* means "telling" and along with being a physical text, the word captures the practice of telling and retelling a story.

Lectio Divina combines slow, conscious reading of a sacred text with contemplation and meditation. The traditional goal is to encourage deeper communication with God through the text and within the reader's life today rather than to find the historical or theological meaning of what was read.

We use this technique to seek a fuller understanding of the meaning of the book, and the prayer of yearning it expresses. When Deb uses this practice with her students, she encourages them to read with a willingness to enter into a text and hear how that text connects to the theme as well as what the text is telling them in that moment, in their particular context.

Lectio Divina is typically done in community with others, and so teachers could either work through the text with their whole class or divide the class up into small groups and give each group a section of text. Because the purpose of Lectio Divina is not to gain information from the text but to use the text as a way to connect with something beyond us, we'll use a short passage from end of the book as an example to focus on. This passage (pages 443–44) is part of Starr's last words to the reader and they sum up her prayer of yearning, of striving toward and landing on hope for what could be in the future. In the passage she talks about Khalil, but also names the many Black people unjustly killed by police and self-styled vigilantes, going back to Emmett Till and others.

Once the teacher and class have chosen this passage to work with, students read the assigned section aloud slowly and deliberately. Encourage students to read it aloud at least twice with a slightly different emphasis each time. Traditionally, a passage is read four times.

Let's look in on a group of four students who have been assigned a short passage from near the end of this longer passage. The teacher asks each member of the group to read their shorter section out loud in turn, and suggests that the group should listen to the words silently each time.

The second step has students reflect on what they just read and heard. The teacher encourages them to pay attention to words that stand out to them and to be aware of any senses, feelings, or imaginations that connect with what was read. What do they visualize? What were the words and phrases trying to convey?

In our example group, one student calls attention to the last two lines of the passage and talks about how she is struck by the resolve in the final words. She says that even though the word "maybe" is in that sentence, it doesn't seem like a "maybe" kind of sentence. Another student points out that the line before that is encouraging since it talks about how we do not fight alone, because there will always be someone else ready to fight. That student says he pictures a huge crowd standing behind Starr, with famous people like Rosa Parks and Dr. King, and John Lewis, but also regular people, some old, some young, all ready to take over if Starr needs them to. A third member of the group asks if the previous student sees himself in that group.

The fourth member of the group changes the focus to concentrate on the earlier part of the passage. She points out that she finds the beginning of the passage comforting, because Starr both has a conviction that things will change, but also doesn't know when or how they will change. This student says that sometimes she really wants to make a difference in the world, but at other times, she feels like there is nothing she can do that will make a difference. She says that Starr's conviction combined with uncertainty is somehow comforting to her.

In the third step, students share with each other words that come to mind or think about them silently. The teacher asks them each to come up with a word that represents how they feel about this passage. They are to say the word out loud, then sit in silence with that word for a moment or two before the next person speaks. In our example group, one person says "Support." After a pause, another says "Conviction." A third person says "Resolve." And the last group member says "Maybe."

We have found that in using this exercise in class, it sometimes works to take a moment or two for students to talk about the words they have selected. In our example group, the last student using the word "Maybe" is interesting. Although it undercuts the direction of the finality of the passage, it also makes room for uncertainty (which does seem to be part of Starr's response, however sure of herself she seems.)

The fourth step of Lectio Divina asks students to reflect quietly on their own about what they read and heard both internally and externally. For this passage, Lectio Divina is an excellent choice because the passage is so emotionally charged. In English classes we tend to want to intellectualize everything we read through discussions of themes and ideas and what everything means. But one reason that we read is to experience what the characters experience. This last step gives our students the chance to live into the emotional experience of the yearning in the book.

This is actually not a new idea. If you have ever read a powerful passage to a class and then, when you finished reading no one said anything and you let students sit with that for a while before anyone spoke, you know what this can feel like, both for the teacher and the students.

The bottom line is that *The Hate U Give*, like many other examples of modern young adult literature, is a powerful book. Our students can handle being entrusted to take in the book for the fullness of what it is: A prayer of yearning.

Chapter 3

Speak and *Long Way Down*
Graphic Novels for Prayers of Anger

Young adult books like *Internment* and *The Hate U Give* both showcase the way young adult protagonists can be awakened to the injustice in their lives and in the world. And in those books, characters are often angry about that injustice. This makes sense. Injustice should make us angry.

While YA novels frequently contain anger (as it is an integral part of adolescence), some novels function as the author's prayer of anger, expressing a response of outrage to a world of injustice and hurt. The methods used to read sacred texts (and particularly the method called PaRDeS) can help students read the novel as a prayer of anger—a cry of injustice thrown out to the universe—and can lead to a further understanding of both the book and the emotions of the reader (or others in the reader's life).

Two graphic novel adaptations of regular text YA books, *Speak* by Laurie Halse Anderson and *Long Way Down* by Jason Reynolds, might be understood as the authors' prayers of anger. Adolescent and young adult readers in general and readers who have suffered trauma in particular can relate to these novels that mirror their own prayers of anger. In fact, there is evidence that reading about the anger of others can function as a kind of bibliotherapy for such readers.

SUMMARY OF *SPEAK*

Speak: The Graphic Novel is based on the 1999 text novel by Laurie Halse Anderson, and later adapted into the graphic novel format by Anderson and illustrator Emily Carroll. Anderson's regular text version won the National Book Award and became the basis of a movie of the same name. *Speak* also became one of the top hundred books to be banned from 2000–2009 according to the American Library Association.

Anderson has written many other young adult novels including *Fever 1793* (2000), *Catalyst* (2002), *Chains* (2008), *Wintergirls* (2009), *Forge* (2010), *The Impossible Knife of Memory* (2014), and *Ashes* (2016).

In the novel, Melinda Sordino is acutely depressed. Her first year at Merryweather High School feels like daily walks through the hallways of hell. The previous summer, Melinda called the cops on Kyle's summer party. Now her former best friend, Rachel, now known as Rachelle, has abandoned her and Melinda has become a social pariah. Melinda finds it easier to be selectively mute, even at home, and can't stop biting her lips until they bleed. She also has started cutting herself. No one hears her cries for help.

To escape the aggressive shunning at school, she finds a janitor's closet and many days hides there for hours. She decorates it with a poster of Maya Angelou, whose books have been banned by the school board. Melinda observes that Angelou must be an excellent writer if she inspires fear in the school board. She also observes fellow student David Petrakis stand up for himself against a racist and xenophobic teacher and admires her art teacher's love of expression and encouragement for students to make mistakes and see beyond the surface of things.

Eventually the source of her depression and anger becomes clear to the reader; it is Andy Evans. Andy Evans raped Melinda at Kyle's party and is now very publicly dating Rachelle. Every time Melinda sees Andy, she is sickened.

Her art teacher, Mr. Freeman, tells her that she needs to express herself or she will die, one piece of herself at a time. David tells her that she can't expect to make a difference in the world unless she speaks for herself. First Melinda tries to find something to care about. She immerses herself in yard work and takes an interest in tennis. She accepts that her art, like herself, cannot be perfect.

True catharsis comes when Melinda borrows a Sharpie and writes a message on the walls of the girl's bathroom warning girls to avoid Andy Evans. Melinda tells Rachelle that Andy Evans raped her at the party. Rachelle is enraged and does not believe her. But when Melinda returns to that bathroom days later, she finds that other girls have added to her warning on the bathroom wall. More graffitied voices let the high school know that Andy Evans is a predator.

Melinda recognizes she is a survivor as she documents her experience in writing. She writes that a small part of her is awakening. When Andy Evans attacks her in the supply closet, she finds her voice and screams. She stumbles into the corridor and tells the lacrosse team to call the cops. She becomes a school hero with hours left in her freshman year. Rachel dumps Andy and reconnects with her. The final line of the graphic novel is the victory of survival in which Melinda says she wants to tell the reader about what happened.

Melinda has the right to be angry. She has been abused by Andy and shunned by her peers, but over the course of the novel, her anger leads her to become a more authentic person who can speak and tell the story of how she survived trauma in order to give hope to others in the same position. Anderson, the author of *Speak*, also survived rape and comforts trauma victims with her writing, offering places and narrative strategies for help to overcome the trauma.

Melinda learns to listen to bold voices around her who dare to speak against the ignorance of teachers, to express her emotions through art, to allow herself to vent through crying. In doing so she is joined by other voices who have been victimized by Andy Evans. She is no longer alone at the end of the graphic novel.

SUMMARY OF *LONG WAY DOWN*

Jason Reynolds wrote *Long Way Down* in 2017 as a regular text novel, then adapted it into a graphic novel with artist Danica Novgorodoff in 2020. The regular text novel won a Newbery Honor, an Edgar Award, a Coretta Scott King Honor, a Printz Honor, and the Walter Dean Myers Award. Reynolds has also written other young adult novels including *All American Boys* (2015), *The Boy in the Black Suit* (2015) and *Look Both Ways* (2019).

In *Long Way Down*, anger runs deep in Will Halloman. His brother Shawn was shot and killed as he was hanging around the neighborhood with Will. A grieving Will reflects on the rules that the men in his life have taught him: that he is not allowed to cry, to snitch on anyone, and that if someone he cares for gets killed, it is his job to find out who did it and kill that person in revenge (p. 30).

One important but wordless panel shows Will grabbing a gun out of a dresser drawer, which he explains is for Rule number 3. Will has three reasons to believe that Carlson Riggs was Shawn's killer, but to the reader, those reasons sound shaky—because of the way turf works for the gangs, because when he watches crime shows, Will can always guess the killer before the police do, and because he has to get revenge (pp. 43–48).

Will gets on an elevator on the eighth floor of his building with the gun. On the seventh floor, a stranger gets on. The stranger introduces himself as Buck. Will recognizes him as the only guy who ever acted like a big brother to Will's brother Shawn. Buck was also the original owner of the gun in Will's back pocket. Buck taught Shawn the rules. But Buck has also been dead for a long time.

On the sixth floor, a fine, young girl enters the elevator. She addresses Will . . . and Buck, which freaks out Will. She appears to know Will quite well. He recognizes her from the playground of his youth when she was shot and killed as they played together when they were children. Her name was Dani. After she was shot, Will cried all night and Shawn taught him Rule No. 1: No crying. Dani tells Will to lose the gun.

On floor five, another stranger enters the elevator. This time it is Will's deceased Uncle Mark, a novice filmmaker. He knew the rules and passed them to his little brother, who was Will and Shawn's father. Uncle Mark sets the scene of how Will might kill Carlson Riggs.

On the fourth floor, Mikey Holloman enters. This is Will's father who died when he was three. Uncle Mark encourages Mikey to tell his story. Mikey followed the rules and shot Uncle Mark's killer. But he killed the wrong guy. Will reflects that his father turns out to not resemble the mental image Will had of him. Will finds that disappointing. Mikey takes Will's gun and holds it to Will's head. The images show Will's intense fear as urine trickles down his legs and onto the elevator floor and he sits hunched in a corner covering his face and wishing for the elevator to reach the lobby while his father puffs on a cigarette.

On floor three, a man named Frick enters. He knows Buck because he killed him. Shawn knew it but didn't rat him out. Shawn killed Frick, as Frick explains. Frick doesn't know Carlson Riggs.

On floor two, a bloody Shawn enters the elevator. Shawn gives him the silent treatment like he used to do when Will annoyed him as a child. Will asks if Riggs was his killer. In response Shawn starts crying. The elevator stops at 09:09:09 a.m. (090909 is also the chemical code for a shade of black paint). Everyone exits except for Will. Shawn finally asks Will if he is coming with them.

The book ends with that question.

HOW READING CAN HELP DEAL WITH ANGER FROM TRAUMA

Anger is part of a human range of emotions, but it can be harmful to mental health. Approximately 20 percent of children in the U.S. report a mental disorder that impacts their daily lives (CDC, 2013). In the U.S. less than a third receive treatment (NCCP, 2014). The Substance Abuse and Mental Health Services Administration notes that children at greatest risk for mental health are least likely to receive services (CDC, 2013). Suicide is the second leading cause of death in the 15–24 age group (CDC, 2013).

One of the ways schools can address mental health issues is through carefully selected young adult texts in which traumatized characters take steps in the direction of wellness. This process, called bibliotherapy, can be an important tool to address anger from trauma.

Rudine Sims Bishop famously observes that books can acts as windows, allowing us to look out at real or imagined worlds. Books can also be sliding glass doors that readers can walk through, using their imaginations, enter and participate in the world that the author has created. Books can also serve as mirrors, allowing readers to see themselves and their lives reflected back to them. Reading affirms readers' identities, and readers often look for mirrors of themselves and windows and doorways into other facets of their identities through books (1990, p. ix).

Some traumatized readers may see themselves in characters who are also dealing with trauma, and the stories may give them the strength and wisdom to deal with their own anger. Other readers may be looking into a situation they have not yet experienced, but may, as a result of reading the book, be able to empathize with the thoughts and actions of others who have been traumatized or avoid becoming angry because of identification with literary story lines.

In bibliotherapy, readers identify with a situation or character, which leads to a catharsis or desire to change, which leads to insight where readers can see their own problems in a new light, allowing for positive change and a new identity. Not only does bibliotherapeutic reading help readers change identities, it also creates gains in attitudes toward reading, reading comprehension, and social emotional competencies (Tijms, Stoop, & Polleck, 2018, p. 525). Bibliotherapy has been described as having four phases: "identification, catharsis and insight" (Lenkowsky, 1987) and a fourth phase of "universalization" (Hebert & Furner, 1997, cited in Lutovac & Kaasila, 2020).

An intervention with African American college students who tended not to seek traditional forms of therapy in spite of being more likely to struggle during college than white students, showed that bibliotherapy increased the participants' intrapersonal intelligence with perspective-taking in relationships (Rawls, Clark, & Hall, 2020).

A study of children and adolescents in foster care showed that bibliotherapy with superhero stories, in which superheroes experienced parental loss, showed gains for their future orientations and goal articulation for college, the military, or to achieve in other areas of life, and a reduction in fantasies about home, with outcomes sustained over time. Betalel and Shechtman (2017) observe, "Superhero bibliotherapy sessions . . . encompass the basic themes of bereavement, trauma, personal tragedy, and strength to heal oneself. They all tell of the hero's quest to find hope and become a positive, useful person—in most cases through altruistic acts" (p. 479).

Bibliotherapy can encourage students to pursue their own heroic character arc in which the best and most interesting of characters have agency to become more powerful through choices that build up themselves and others, often at the same time.

Bibliotherapy as a way to read allows people to grow emotionally, and promotes effective change, as readers process their own emotions as they read about characters with similar experiences (Lenkowsy, 1987). It has been used to help teachers-in-training identify with students (Lutovac & Kaasila, 2020), but it depends upon the right books being selected. As Lutovac and Kaasila (2020) observe, "the selected readings (should) correspond with a child's feelings, needs, interests and goals; must successfully resolve or cope with a fear; and should take into account the child's gender and background" (p. 484).

Teachers cannot do the one-on-one counseling of trained mental health experts, but they can use some counseling techniques to illuminate how characters change and grow. Books selected for bibliotherapy should evoke emotions, provoke identification with characters and story lines, and provide vicarious experiences for students (Lutovac & Kaasila 2020, p. 493). Even some training in bibliotherapy allows teachers to develop basic skills, sometimes serve as unofficial counselors when teaching literature, use books to increase cultural awareness, and use books to increase knowledge of other cultures (Joubert & Hay, 2019).

There is a difference between therapy done by a trained counselor and what literature teachers do to open deep conversations with students who have multiple experiences and multiple points of view using the steps of bibliotherapy in a more general way. For students who have been physically violated or have experienced death through violence, *Speak* and *Long Way Down* can function as the authors' prayers of anger and allow readers to identify with protagonists and start to rebuild their lives.

Literature allows us to see life problems with a certain amount of distance because the stories we read are not about us (Deitcher, 2019, p. 18). As Rosenblatt describes, literature places our life's problems outside ourselves so that we can see them clearly from a detached distance. This allows us to understand our motivations and our context more objectively (Rosenblatt, 1968, p. 41).

Both *Speak* and *Long Way Down* are good choices for bibliotherapy because they connect to the experiences many adolescents have had in being violated physically and also to the generational trauma that African Americans face in a country that enslaved them and still often views them as lesser or other. These experiences reflect the passion and pain behind recent social movements such as Me Too and Black Lives Matter. The best bibliotherapeutic books reflect the world adolescents live in.

Advocates of bibliotherapy in Jewish education observe that sacred texts can be read with a bibliotherapeutic lens. They argue that readers should make connections with characters and actions in sacred texts. Nechama Leibowitz observes, "We must never allow the study of Biblical figures to be distorted into a simplistic story devoid of meaning and relevance to our everyday lives" (1941, p. 3). It is important for teachers to share such a lens with the reading of literature that connects the text to relevant aspects of the lives of adolescents.

This requires exegesis or personally unpacking texts for meaning. As Deitcher (2019) observes,

> a central tenet in teaching Jewish texts is the firmly rooted principle of Jewish exegesis and its coveted role in this learning. The canonical texts invite the reader to actively explore myriad diverse and oftentimes conflicting interpretations. This empowers the reader with a weighty sense of responsibility in the learning experience. . . . Furthermore, a key feature of the bibliotherapy approach is the portrayal of literary characters in ways that are compelling for the reader. (p. 19)

Readers are thus encouraged to contemplate the actions of the literary figures in ways that help them better understand their own thoughts, feelings, and behaviors. Bibliotherapy works only when readers take an active role in reading and make text-to-self connections with characters and their insights for positive change. Texts such as *Speak* and *Long Way Down* can mirror students' journeys by showing them the authors' prayers of anger.

Researchers have suggested that literacy has "been an act of resistance that is liberating and mentally healing" (Ford, Walters, Byrd, & Harris, 2018, p. 54). For African Americans, this has been particularly true. In the times of slavery, enslaved persons were prohibited from learning to read and write (Williams, 2009). Reading became a heroic act of pushing back against the cruelty of the time. As Ford and others note, "Therapeutic reading has been and continues to be a technique individuals and therapists use to understand, escape from, push through, or acquire a solution for adverse circumstances" (2018, p. 55). It can be a powerful tool for working through anger.

Bibliotherapy starts with reading and leads to reflecting on the messages of stories "that can draw participants into a process of reflection, in ways that are user friendly and non-threatening" (Deitcher, 2019, p. 17). Bibliotherapy is meant to help the reader have deep understandings of life. Anger is a part of life that is often poorly understood.

Zoran (2000) suggests the following model for interpreting text with a bibliotherapeutic lens:

To begin with, readers should observe the plurality of meaning in texts. Next, the reader should participate creatively by actively reading and understanding the problem and the character. Then readers should acknowledge that they bring their own ideas, preconceptions, and learning to the reading and allow those to be known. Finally, readers must understand that interpretations are shaped by "social, historical, and cultural norms." (p. 21)

PaRDeS is a great pedagogical organizer for cathartic discussions because, like bibliotherapy, PaRDeS offers steps toward insight when readers put themselves in the shoes of protagonists and use literature as mirrors, windows, and sliding glass doors. Additionally, PaRDeS offers a framework for getting at the complexity of anger, how it affects many people throughout the text, how the anger came to be, and what it could turn into.

USING PaRDeS TO DISCUSS *SPEAK* AND *LONG WAY DOWN*

PaRDeS is a mnemonic for an approach to interpretation of sacred text that extends back to Judaic tradition in the Middle Ages. PaRDeS stands for *Peshat* (surface), *Remez* (hints at deep meaning), *Derash* (inquire or seek) and *Sod* (secret). It is a way of coming back to the same passage repeatedly and thinking about it in different ways.

But how can we use PaRDeS to discuss graphic novels like *Speak* and *Long Way Down*? In our version, class members nominate a significant panel or two from the graphic novel being studied (from a particular chapter or, if time is short, from the entire book). The class selects a single nominated panel or two to discuss at a time. Then the class discusses the surface meaning of the selected panel or panels and what they see there, considering (in the case of the theme we have chosen) evidence of anger, the effects of anger, the causes of anger, or anything else that takes their attention regarding the theme.

Next, the class picks the most important word in a speech balloon or expository sentence in the panel, or identifies the most important visual motif, and traces all other occurrences of that word or image elsewhere in the novel and discusses what those other occurrences reveal.

The third step is for the class to ask themselves what lesson they can take from that sentence or image that connects to their own experiences or perceptions about the world.

Finally, the class considers whether the passage has a secret to offer them and what that secret might mean. This question gives them permission to really reach for an interpretation or connection that might seem like a stretch (but might, after some discussion, prove to be more solid than they thought).

The teacher might then ask each group to share the most important insight they got out of their discussion. As with the other approaches, this could easily be adapted to be used in small groups or partner groups.

BIBLIOTHERAPEUTIC PaRDeS

The first step of applying PaRDeS to bibliotherapy is for the teacher or students to select a panel from the text that offers potential for identification with a character's trauma. As the teachers who have taught both texts, we have selected page 371 of *Speak*, an unusual page because it does not contain bordered panels but is simply an illustration filling up the entire page. The foreground contains a tree offering an outline to the page. Within the branches of the tree, two birds fly in the clouds. In the text, Melinda states that the icy feeling within her melts away and pieces of ice fall to the floor and evaporate in a patch of sunlight.

The pages before the image give it context. This image of melting is one that she draws in art class during a timed exam. She cries as she draws. Mr. Freeman admonishes her to stop crying before the salt in her tears ruins the art supplies. Melinda explains to the reader that her tears are breaking apart the last chunk of ice in her throat. Mr. Freeman sympathizes, acknowledging that she has probably been through a lot of difficulty. The image in the panel we have selected graphically reinforces Mr. Freeman's observation: Melinda *has* been through a lot.

The panel we selected from *Long Way Down* is taken from the end of the graphic novel. Shawn, bloodied from his gunshot wound, has entered the elevator. He has not spoken to Will. Will is looking at his brother beseechingly. The text describes how there is a sound like machinery and cables and gears scraping and turning and squealing as if the elevator is moaning in pain, except that the sound is coming from Shawn's belly. Shawn doesn't say a word to Will, he just makes those sounds as the elevator stops abruptly. A word balloon at the bottom of the page indicates that the elevator makes a dinging sound.

This page also has no panel borders. It is clear from the previous page that Shawn is crying even though it is against the rules. This is the moment: weeping is appropriate for the loss experienced.

The second stage is applying the step of *remez*, which means hint, by looking for other examples of the motifs of trees or crying in both books as understanding that catharsis is needed. Catharsis, relief from strong emotions, can include crying, artistic expression as an outlet for anger from trauma, including storytelling and drawing. Catharsis starts with the truth that the motif noted in the shot represents pain for the protagonist.

In *Speak*, illustrator Emily Carroll draws a black tree edged with a black border on the cover of the book. White space allows the branches to be outlined. One green leaf in shiny foil remains on the tree. Melinda's green face on the trunk anthropomorphizes the tree. The back cover is black. Here the branches of the tree are white space. Three words in white on the back cover page declare that Melinda said no. We see hints that Melinda is going to tell her story and continue to live and not die.

In *Long Way Down* the first instance of crying is a full page spread on the page where Will and Shawn's mother holds Shawn after he has been shot. She cries repeatedly that she does not want it to be her baby and asks why this happened. Will notes in the exposition that if your family blood is also inside someone else, you never want to see their blood outside of their body. This serves as a hint for Will as the book ends with his indecision: will he leave the elevator and shoot someone who is probably the wrong guy, or will he go back upstairs and comfort his mother who does not deserve to lose her whole family through violence?

The step of *derash* involves some work with the text as students trace all instances where trees or references to crying appear in both books. The purpose for bibliotherapeutic practice is to offer insight for change. In *Speak*, we see Melinda surrounded by two trees before Mr. Freeman tells every student in his art class to study the word on the paper he has handed them. The word tells them that their assignment for the year is to figure out how to turn that word into art. They are allowed to sculpt, draw, carve, ink, paint, or experiment in whatever way they wish until they figure out how to make their art express something of themselves, convey an emotion, and generally speak to every person that sees it.

Melinda's word is, of course, "tree." Students should find and carefully consider the moments when trees appear in the graphic novel either in word or image. We count about forty such images of trees, functioning as images of trauma and healing as Melinda draws trees throughout the year and finds well-being in doing so. She realizes she can grow and prosper like a tree even though trees surrounded her during her rape. When we ask student-readers which images of trees take their attention and why, they may come to this conclusion or discover insights that we had not noticed.

Students might make connections in *Long Way Down* between the different times that crying comes up in the book. Will's mother weeps after Shawn is shot but Will cannot because Rule No. 1 means no crying. Shawn taught him the rule after he cried when Dani was shot as they played together on the playground.

When his father gets on the elevator, Will wants to cry and tell him about Shawn, but he can't. He does, however pee on himself when his father points the gun to his head. But then Shawn gets on the elevator and begins to weep, Will cries for the first time since childhood. As everyone leaves the elevator, Will lingers. Shawn asks him if he is coming along with them, leaving the reader to wonder if Will has changed his mind about revenge. The reader must do the cognitive work based on what they have just witnessed in images and words.

A fourth phase of bibliotherapy involves *universalization* or learning from the truth of others. This corresponds with the final step of PaRDeS, called *sod*, meaning "mystery." Some people understand the term because they have experienced the mystery of allowing anger to morph into something wonderful. For *Speak*, one *sod* might involve the other young women who added to Melinda's message about Andy Evans on the bathroom wall, letting the world anonymously know about a predator in their school. These messages offer hope for Melinda in her trauma. They also stand in for others like Maya Angelou, a victim of rape, who also muted herself until she found the courage to inspire others through her writing.

For Will, the *sod* is revealed in pieces as each new person enters the elevator and shows Will that the rules do not work and that they were responsible for the deaths of many of his loved ones. Another mystery is how the elevator keeps going down. Perhaps this is a way of understanding Will's emotional state, but it could also be a metaphor for the cycle of killing—the elevator admits more and more people whose lives have been ruined and keeps plummeting lower and lower. Perhaps the mystery is when Will can get off the elevator and how to turn things around. Maybe Will needs a new set of rules to document the stories of the dead in order to bring about real change.

TRANSFORMING ANGER THROUGH READING

An employee wellness guide for faculty and staff at University of California, Berkeley notes that people respond to anger in four basic ways: aggressively (like Will when he gets a gun from his bureau to exact revenge), passively (like Melinda's silence and isolation), passively/aggressively (also like Melinda when she despises her classmates and family for not understanding her needs and responding with silence, isolation, and harsh judgements because they lack knowledge of her trauma), and assertively when the anger is managed and communicated (such as when Melinda writes about Andy Evans on the bathroom wall and then, in a later scene, finds her voice and screams, turning him in) (Understanding Anger, n.d.).

It is important for readers to determine how Will and Melinda respond to anger and note how they as readers respond to anger and then to determine the most positive ways to deal with anger.

Tools include stress reduction by social bonding with those who care about them, or talk therapy. Melinda does have safe people in her life like Mr. Freeman. When she talks to him, she grows in insight. David, her classmate, also expresses an interest in her personal well-being; he shows her how to speak up. Will trusts his mother; this would be a time to spend time talking to her as they both have experienced tremendous loss.

Handling anger by recognizing it and working through it is a life skill. Perpetual anger damages mental health. Aggressive responses hurt others and things, allowing anger to control the angered rather than giving them power to control anger. As readers read both graphic novels, they can learn to manage their anger (or understand the anger of others) and learn from the struggles, missed opportunities, and possible triumphs in Melinda and Will's stories.

Chapter 4

Confession in *Goodbye Days*

We have seen in the previous chapters the way in which young adult literature can function as prayers of lament, yearning, and anger. In this chapter we will explore how rich and robust a discussion can be when we examine a whole YA book as a type of prayer.

The word *confession* brings up many different images: a scene from a movie with a priest hearing a confession in a dark and mysterious booth or a moment in childhood when the guilt stemming from a wrong action resulted in an eventual embarrassed admission to parents. Many confessions are matters that seem important at the time, but in retrospect are not necessarily things that ultimately changed someone else's world.

But other moments of confession revolve around bigger mistakes, bigger offenses, and sometimes confessing them is more than a single simple discussion In *Goodbye Days*, a 2017 YA novel by Jeff Zentner, Carver Briggs may have caused the deaths of his three best friends. And Carver's struggle to confess that mistake and begin to heal is the focus of the story.

Goodbye Days was nominated for the Lincoln Prize, selected for the Louisiana Young Reader's Choice Master List, selected for the Texas TAYSHAS High School Reading List, selected for the Virginia Capitol Choices Award List, and was awarded the Carolyn W. Field Award and the Westchester Fiction Award. Zentner's other work has won the New York Times Notable Book Award, ALAN's Walden Award, and the International Literacy Association Award. His books are used in many high school classrooms in the United States and abroad.

Zentner has written other young adult novels including *The Serpent King* (2016), *Rayne and Delilah's Midnight Matinee* (2019), and *In the Wild Light* (2021).

The story of *Goodbye Days* centers on Carver, who sends a text to his friend Mars, even though he knows Mars is driving his other friends, Blake and Eli, home from a movie. Carver sends a text asking them where they are and asking them to text back. He sends the text to his friend Mars because he is most likely to reply. When Carver finds out that Blake, Eli, and Mars have been killed in a car accident that his text may have been fully or partly responsible for, he is racked with guilt. He wants to talk to someone about it, but finds that with his best friends dead and his sister leaving for college, he has no one to tell.

Then the police find Carver's text on Mars's phone. Mars's dad, a judge, puts pressure on the police to open an investigation, and soon Carver and his parents are meeting with a lawyer who tells him not to talk with anyone at all about the accident. That becomes harder when Carver develops a friendship with Eli's girlfriend who is also grieving.

And then Blake's grandma asks Carver if he will join her for a "goodbye day." Since she never had a chance to have a final day with the grandson she raised, she wonders if Carver would be willing to be a stand-in for Blake. They go fishing, have breakfast at a Waffle House, play pranks on people the way Blake always did, and finish the day with Blake's favorite dinner. Both Carver and Nana Betsy laugh a lot and cry a lot and Carver feels a bit better.

However, when Eli's parents demand their own goodbye day, Carver has a much more difficult time. Eli's parents are separating and getting a divorce and Carver is unsure how much they blame him. Close on the heels of that disastrous goodbye day, Judge Frederick Edwards, who blames Carver for his son Mars's death, also wants a goodbye day. Carver soon realizes that this will not be a time of remembrance, or even passive-aggressive guilting, but more likely anger, venting, and making Carver pay for Mars's death

In our discussions about how a book can function as the author's prayer, we have discussed several examples already, and, to be sure, some books embody that notion of YA novel as prayer more completely than others. *Goodbye Days* is remarkably rich in that regard. This chapter will illustrate how completely a book can function as a prayer, in this case, a prayer of confession.

The theme of confession in this novel is not a hard one to spot. But often the discussions teachers try to initiate after students have read a young adult novel consist of brainstorming various themes and perhaps calling upon the students to identify passages that contain the word "confession." Sometimes even the word *theme* becomes synonymous with a single-word response.

But to say that a theme is a single word is to vastly oversimplify that theme. YA books like *Goodbye Days* explore multiple facets and perspectives of a single theme. Instead of looking for students to provide a one-word theme, it might be more helpful to have them express the theme as a more complete thought. Unfortunately, requiring students to state a theme as a sentence doesn't solve the problem either.

For example, saying that the theme of *Goodbye Days* is that "Confession is difficult" or "Confession brings relief" or "Confession is inevitable" still limits what the book is really about. Perhaps having students state a theme as a question would help ("Does confession lead to resolution of guilt?"). This might be particularly effective if we are thinking in terms of the thematic content of a book consisting of multiple questions.

What we are suggesting in this book is that, instead of trying to name a single theme as if we have captured the meaning of the book, a better way to take advantage of the multiple perspectives students bring to our classrooms, and the way in which discussion can air everyone's ideas about the purposes or value of confession and bring new insights to everyone without needing to limit the ground a novel can cover, might be to look to the text of the book. And the text of *Goodbye Days* has a lot to give.

CARVER'S GUILT IN *GOODBYE DAYS*

The theme of struggling with the tension between wanting to confess and wanting to escape from confession is present from the beginning of the novel. The very first line spoken by Carver, the first-person narrator, directly to the audience explains that the main character's actions may have taken the lives of his three best friends (p. 1). It is a startling way to open a book, but as a confession it is not particularly strong.

The confession of guilt is qualified in two ways. First, the actual sentence includes the word *may*. This is certainly not an unequivocal confession. At the same time, under the bravado, we can sense deep anxiety.

Carver goes on to introduce the main characters in this story—Blake Lloyd's grandma Nana Betsy; Eli Bauer's parents; Eli's twin Adair; and Mars's dad—Judge Frederick Edwards—and explains how each of them feels about his guilt.

Then Carver introduces himself, saying that he believes that his actions killed his friends. This seems like a real confession, except that immediately afterwards he qualifies it, saying it was not deliberate on his part, and he also believes that no one else thinks he did it deliberately either. And then on the next page he backs off even further, saying he is not absolutely certain that it was his text that killed them (p. 3). Through this entire chapter, Carver wavers, feeling uncertain of whether he has done anything worth confessing.

After the first funeral, Blake's, Carver talks with Jesmyn, who was Eli's girlfriend. She is kind to him, and they agree to talk again later. Carver is glad to talk to someone who shares his grief. At the same time, he is worried that she blames him. He suspects that he is letting himself assume that, since she has been kind to him, that she doesn't think Eli's death was Blake's fault. He admits, however, that it is possible that she is being kind in order to convince herself not to hate him (p. 21).

Later at Nana Betsy's house, after the funeral, Carver is so racked with guilt and shame that he has to force each bite of food down his throat, which feels constricted. He concludes that he is unworthy of the food (p. 29). Carver is not only suffering the pain of grief, but also the more intense pain of guilt. In fact, his guilt is so great that he begins to wonder about whether he will be punished eternally for what he did.

Carver describes himself as someone who believes in God in a casual way (p. 35). He explains that his family goes to church maybe four or five times per year and that his dad has enough faith that he suffers for it, but not enough faith to try to make others suffer too (p. 35). Carver wonders whether his friends are in some sort of afterlife, and worries that there might be hell where they are in pain and being punished. He wonders if he will go to hell for killing his friends. He worries that Nana Betsy might not have the power to forgive him or that her forgiveness might not matter (p. 35).

Carver's increasing guilt leads to a panic attack when he tries to return to school the next day. His guilt and stress increase again when Judge Edwards announces at a press conference that he has asked detectives to open an investigation to determine if Carver is culpable for the deaths of his friends. Then a reporter calls and leaves a message asking for Caver to comment on the accident for a story about the Judge's announcement. Carver doesn't tell his parents and doesn't call the reporter back. He wonders what he would say other than expressing that he does not want to go to prison, even though he worries that maybe he deserves it (p. 55).

SEEKING RELIEF FROM GUILT

Anyone reading this analysis might wonder if this novel is only an endless waterfall of guilty feelings. It is not. Zentner gives us Carver's vivid memories of his friends and descriptions of the support his sister and his parents give him.

Carver also escapes the weight of guilt when talking on the phone with Jesmyn, his deceased friend Eli's girlfriend. Both of them are grieving and it feels good to talk with someone who knows what he is going through. They talk late into the night, and at some point, Carver starts to feel something like absolution—the feeling one gets when one has been forgiven. Toward the end of the talk, Carver finds that the weight of guilt that he carries is lessening as they talk (p. 59). But this feeling is fleeting. Within a page or so, all of Carver's guilt and anxiety seem to return.

Perhaps to get the feeling back, Carver goes to Blake's Nana Betsy's house. When he had talked with her after the funeral, she had mentioned that Blake had always helped her weed her garden. Carver has come to weed the garden in his place. She tells him that weeding is unnecessary. She says she can hire a kid from the neighborhood to do the weeding. She welcomes him in.

But Carver protests, saying that he needs to do it.

Nana Betsy softly tells him that he doesn't need to.

Carver again says that he does need to. Then he feels like he might start crying so he turns away from her (p. 64).

Carver needs relief from the crushing guilt he feels, and hopes that by working for Blake's grandma, by doing this penance, he will feel some sort of solace. Immediately after the exchange quoted above, Carver wants to tell her about the detectives and the possible investigation, but he decides not to because he cannot bear her thinking of him as a criminal. So while he seeks the relief of penance, he also finds himself turning toward confession and then away from it.

While Carver works, Nana Betsy prepares lunch for them. Over tomato sandwiches, they retell stories about Blake and find themselves laughing. Carver discovers, "For a moment, I don't feel guilty anymore. The smallest taste of redemption. And it is sweet on my tongue" (p. 67). Shortly after that, Nana Betsy proposes the first of the goodbye days. Nana Betsy proposes they get together and combine their memories of Blake to have a day in which they both share Blake with each other for one more day (p. 68).

This would seem to be just what the doctor ordered for Carver, but he is hesitant. He feels like he is running to his car with something he shoplifted and the store's security person is shouting for him to return (p. 68). Carver doesn't feel like he deserves relief. Later, while talking to Jesmyn, he tells her how his mom told him that overcoming grief takes time and that there isn't a pill you can take to make everything feel better. Then Carver thinks to himself that even if there were such a pill, he doubts he would let himself take it. He figures he would feel like he didn't deserve it (p. 80).

The next day, when he is at a park with Jesmyn, Carver confesses that he had a panic attack recently (p. 82). *Confess* is the term that Carver uses. While he could have used the word *admits* or *reveals*, it is *confession* that is on his mind. Of course, his panic attack is not what he really wants to confess.

Later in the same conversation, he tells Jesmyn that Nana Betsy asked him to do a goodbye day. When Jesmyn asks if he is going to do it, he says he is not sure, but then realizes that he really wants to tell Jesmyn how he hungers to be absolved of what he has done. But he realizes that if he did so, he would be admitting that he is guilty and that has to remain his secret (p. 84). Carver wants to be absolved of guilt, but he can't be absolved until he confesses what he is guilty of. And that is the catch. As long as he is unwilling to admit to her what he has done, it is impossible for anyone to absolve him of that guilt.

His pain is so strong that Carver decides to do the goodbye day with Nana Betsy. He drives to her house, parks, walks to her door. And then he chickens out. He is afraid that she will see in his facial expression that he is a coward and that she will be able to smell how guilty he is. So he sneaks away and hopes that Nana Betsy will forget that she ever asked him (p. 89).

As his desire to confess his crime grows, so do the barriers against that confession. When Mars's dad, Judge Edwards, holds a press conference and announces that he is requesting that the district attorney (DA) open an investigation into the deaths of the three boys, Carver's mom and dad hire a lawyer. In the lawyer's office, Carver gives a kind of a confession. Under the lawyer's questioning, Carver recounts the text he sent to Mars even though he knew that Mars was driving and likely to text him back. The lawyer, Mr. Krantz, offers neither absolution nor reassurance nor penance.

Instead, he warns Carver not to talk to anyone about the accident unless Mr. Krantz is present (p. 97). He commands Carver not to confess. More than that, he seems to imply by this prohibition, that confession will result in Carver putting his freedom at risk. So, this is not about Carver doing the right thing to honor his friends, it is about saving his own skin.

After Carver's panic attack at school, his sister encourages him to see the counselor who helped her, Dr. Mendez. This seems like an obvious opportunity for Carver to confess his fears of culpability in his friends' deaths. But although he finds Dr. Mendez easy to talk to, he is reluctant to bring up the accident, At one point Dr. Mendez asks Carver if he has had any reflections on the grief that he has been feeling.

To Carver, this is an easy question, and yet he finds himself unable to answer it. He wants to confess to Dr. Mendez and Carver finds that Dr. Mendez seems like he would not judge Carver. But Carver vacillates between trusting and not trusting Dr. Mendez. On the one hand, Caver wants to tell Dr. Mendez how his friends' deaths are like a weight around his neck, and on the other hand, he doesn't want to risk Dr. Mendez being disappointed in him (p. 141).

In the end, Carver just says that he misses his friends. Even though Dr. Mendez has explained about professional confidentiality, and even though it would be safe to do so, Dr. Mendez is not who Carver needs to confess to. And his grief continues, unabated, as does his guilt. Carver is plagued by what he calls "what-ifs" and "do-overs" when he is drifting off to sleep. He imagines what it would be like if he didn't text Mars, or if he had been able to keep them from going to the movie in the first place (p. 169).

He consciously doesn't imagine, though, what his friends might have done differently. He reasons that since he was not with them, and since he had no influence over what they did, he cannot imagine their actions, or the actions of the semi truck driver. He can only control what he does. And all he really needs to do is an absence of action. He just has to not text (p. 170). But this doesn't give Carver any relief from his guilt. There is no relief.

THE FIRST GOODBYE DAY WITH NANA BETSY AND THE BEGINNINGS OF REAL CONFESSION

And finally the day comes when Carver will spend the day with Nana Betsy, remembering his friend Blake. They start the day off with fishing because even though Blake and his grandma never caught anything, they did laugh a lot. Carver thinks he had prepared himself for this experience, but he finds himself wanting to confess to Nana Betsy and tell her why he doesn't deserve this day. Then he remembers his lawyer's warning. He manages only a partial confession, telling Nana Betsy that he is not sure he should be part of such a special day (p. 184).

But Zentner is not only exploring Carver's need for confession, he is also exploring how people react to that confession. Nana Betsy is firm in her response, but it is also a response of forgiveness on some level. She tells him that, indeed, they are doing the most special thing they could possibly do, and that it is Nana Betsy who gets to determine who is worthy to have that experience with her. She tells him that she has decided that he is worthy and that is the end of the discussion. Carver describes her tone as kind, but also with a kind of no-nonsense edge (p. 184).

Nana Betsy is, on some level, not only welcoming Carver into the goodbye day, but also giving him a kind of blanket forgiveness. Whether or not he is really worthy of taking part in the goodbye day in his eyes, or even in some sort of objective sense, is not the point, she is saying. This is her choice, and she chooses to include Carver regardless of his own feelings of inadequacy.

But Carver is not ready for this yet. He shakes his head and still fears that even though Nana Betsy is generous, it isn't enough to free him of his guilt (p. 184).

Nana Betsy tells him how she uprooted her life and moved to Nashville so Blake could go to school there, and how she is so glad that the move resulted in Blake meeting Carver and the others. In a flash, Carver has a realization and nearly blurts out that the risk Nana Betsy took in moving also resulted, in a way, in Blake dying. If she had not brought Blake to Nashville, he wouldn't have been in the car crash (p. 185). Carver doesn't say that though, instead he asks her if she regrets making the move. Nana Betsy responds with a negative, explaining that if Blake hadn't come to Nashville and the school, he would never have lived.

Carver is still dancing around the confession that part of him wants to make and part of him doesn't. And so, he tries to confess something different. After Nana Betsy recounts how her daughter Mitzi, Blake's mom, raised Blake in a filthy, trash-strewn trailer, how Mitzi's drug and alcohol addiction resulted in Blake being neglected severely, and how Nana Betsy rescued him at gunpoint from her daughter and took him away so he might have a chance to be raised in love, Carver has a clear memory of a time he was hanging out in his house with Blake and when he was impatient with his mom. Blake asked him why he was so mean to his mom.

Carver told Blake that he didn't understand. Blake replied that if he were in Carver's place and had a mom like Carver's, he would never be unkind to her. Blake told Carver that he didn't know how lucky he was, but Blake knew. Carver tells Nana Betsy that he is ashamed of how he treated his mom when Blake was there (p. 189).

But while this is a confession of sorts, Nana Betsy does not offer forgiveness or absolution. She just says that she is not judging Carver. Nana Betsy has been hospitable, and she shows every indication that she is quick to forgive, but the small test confession that Carver has just made is a confession of a time he was rude to his mother, not toward Nana Betsy. This is not for her to forgive.

Carver keeps circling back around to wanting to bring up his actions that may have contributed to the death of her grandson. When Nana Betsy tells him that, now that Blake is gone, she intends to sell her house and move to Chattanooga to be closer to her other children, Carver considers how, in a way, he is responsible for Nana Betsy's move too. And so he says he is sorry.

Nana Betsy tells him there is no reason to apologize because she is glad to be going home. Carver reiterates that he is sorry for forcing her to move. Nana Betsy tells him again that he has nothing to apologize for (p. 190).

One can imagine a long pause between when Carver says he is sorry and when he says for forcing her to move. Carver sees the text he sent which may have caused the accident as rippling out and disrupting people's lives, in this case, Nana Betsy's. So her reassurance that it is not his fault, to Carver is only because she does not understand the whole picture. He thinks that he doesn't need to say he is sorry. He believes that at best he came very close to committing negligent homicide but he can't tell anybody except Dr. Mendez and Mr. Kranz. He reasons that it is his guilt that makes him have to be so careful about who he tells, and without that guilt he could speak freely (p. 190).

After Nana Betsy leaves their two new fishing poles by the lake with a note giving them away to whoever finds them in honor of her grandson Blake, they go to a Waffle House restaurant for breakfast. Nana Betsy talks about how she believes in heaven, the Christian afterlife, and hopes to see Blake again when she dies. Then Carver again feels a yearning to confess. He asks Nana Betsy what actions she thinks would keep someone from going to heaven. Nana Betsy holds his gaze and asks him what he means. Carver asks her what happens if God holds him accountable for the accident (p. 194).

While this is not precisely a confession in that it is a question rather than a statement of guilt, Carver has finally conveyed to Nana Betsy that he fears he may be responsible for her grandson's death. Rather than responding with anger or reassurance, Nana Betsy instead answers the question, saying that her God judges someone based on their whole life and on their whole heart. She says that if God makes people walk on a tightrope across the flames of damnation, then she doesn't think it is worth it to praise him for eternity. If that is what God is like, she would rather jump from the rope into the flames (p. 194–95).

This does not satisfy Carver. He has the answer to his question, but since he doesn't share Nana Betsy's belief system, at least not completely, her answer seems relative to him. It comforts her, but not him.

When Nana Betsy later, in the car, comments on how Blake never found the right girl, Carver realizes that Blake never told her that he was gay. Now Carver feels a responsibility and gently tells Nana Betsy this for Blake. Nana Betsy is only upset that Blake never told her. Then she asks Carver if he would play act with her that moment of Blake's coming out, in which Carver would play Blake. Carver agrees. When Carver-as-Blake tells her, it feels like a different sort of confession. Nana Betsy's response is less to Carver and more to Blake, though. As if she is speaking to Blake, she says fiercely that Blake's being gay doesn't make any difference at all to her. She loves him more than anything, including God. She says that if God has a problem with Blake's sexuality, God can talk to her about it because she loves Blake for who he is (p. 204).

Carver gets his moment of confession and his moment of absolution, but it isn't for him. It is for one of the friends he feels responsible for possibly killing. But this gives him courage, and a page later, in spite of his lawyer's advice, he finds himself explaining about the panic attacks, his counselor, and then, with a dry mouth and feeling a bit lightheaded, Carver tells Nana Betsy that he has learned that the DA is thinking of pressing charges against Carver for the accident (p. 205). Nana Betsy turns from the stove, her mouth open. Carver quietly tells her that Mars's dad, the judge, asked the DA to determine if there are any charges that can be brought against Carver (p. 206).

Nana Betsy is astonished when Carver explains that he might be charged for negligent homicide, He explains that if the DA can provide evidence that he was texting Mars, knew that Mars was driving, knew that it would be likely that Mars would text him back, and that Carver also knew that driving while texting was unsafe, that the DA might be able to charge Carver with negligent homicide (p. 206). Nana Betsy points out that Carver didn't know all of that at the time. When he is silent, she realizes that perhaps he did know. That moment of silence is Carver's confession. And although he could not get out the words, he has admitted that his actions may have caused the death of Nana Betsy's grandson, the person she loved the most in the world.

When he does break his silence, Carver explains that the only really solid evidence that the DA would have is if he confessed. The DA can't force him to confess, so the only real danger is if he confesses to someone else. Carver has, at this point, given Nana Betsy the power to extract revenge, to make him pay for contributing to Blake's death. With one phone call to Judge Edwards or the detectives on the case, she could testify and put Carver in jail.

In confessing, Carver has accepted responsibility for his actions but he also knows that he may have just made a massive mistake. Emotionally, however, he feels relief, which he compares to the feeling of pulling off a scab. He concludes that it is strange how he could feel pleasure from potentially destroying himself. The reader might question whether the pleasure he feels has more to do with putting himself in harm's way or in accepting the responsibility that he has wanted to accept for most of the book at this point.

Nana Betsy, after a pause to batter the chicken that they will be eating later, responds, but it is not a response of anger or glee at being able to get revenge. Instead she declares that she supposes that their conversation never occurred. It is a gracious response. She is offering to erase the confession as if it were a mistake. And all Carver would need to do is change the subject and he could escape.

But he doesn't do that. Instead, he tells her she doesn't need to lie for him. He tells her that he deserves punishment (p. 207). While the reader might suspect that Carver does not deserve to be punished to the extent he might be thinking of, it is also clear that he is willing to take the punishment he believes is due.

Nana Betsy's response is to imply that she has no idea what lie he is talking about. Her answer is comical in her persistence to erase the conversation, but also makes it clear that, if Carver is not wavering in his position, neither is she. Carver plows ahead, explaining that this is the reason he feels like he does not deserve the time he has spent with her (and possibly implies that he does not deserve her letting him off the hook as well). If Carver is unsure of whether he deserves punishment, he is also unsure whether he deserves the grace Nana Betsy is giving him.

Carver puts his face in his hands and admits that he is ashamed of himself. He hates himself because of his actions. And now he has confessed out loud, not only that his actions may have killed his friends, but to the related offense of hating himself (though he may not see hating himself as an offense, but perhaps as a consequence.) Nana Betsy takes his hands and pulls them away from his face. She holds his hands tightly. He looks away, feeling his face burning with shame. Then Nana Betsy tells him that maybe he made a mistake, but that the accident needs to have a survivor. She says that Carver owes it to Blake to survive.

And in that moment, holding Carver's hands, she acknowledges his confession, identifies it as a mistake, and recognizes the error in what Carver did. She also, however, begins to absolve him of his guilt, She points out that even though Blake had been neglected by his mother horribly, he never put blame on her for his life. So Nana Betsy makes it clear that, while she will acknowledge the wrong, she will neither judge nor blame him.

Chapter 24, in which all of this occurs, is one of the longest chapters in the book and contains a lot of scenes worth discussing. While Nana Betsy and Carver enjoy Blake's favorite meal of cornbread-encrusted fried chicken, Nana Betsy asks Carver for a favor. Would he stay with her while she calls Blake's mother Mitzi (Nana Betsy's daughter)? She has to tell her that her son, whom she neglected, whom Nana Betsy took from her, has died. Carver agrees and soon finds himself standing next to her as she dials the phone. But when she has Mitzi on the end of the phone, Nana Betsy cannot say the words.

Carver takes the phone and tells Mitzi that her son died in a car accident, that they had the funeral, that they are sorry they were unable to reach her (Nana Betsy had to hire a private detective to get Mitzi's phone number). Mitzi demands to speak with her mom again and asks Carver to put her back on the phone. She blames Nana Betsy for taking Blake away and she blames her for his death (p. 222). Carver refuses, fearing Mitzi will just yell at Nana Betsy.

And then, as Mitzi cries, Carver tells her that it is not her fault. He starts to tell her that it is nobody's fault, but then he confesses once again, telling her that it is his fault and that he is the one she can yell at. Mitzi wails on the phone that Carver let Blake get hurt. She accuses him of not taking care of Blake (though she may be including Nana Betsy in that "You." Carver's only response to her is that he knows.)

He has confessed again, this time to Blake's birth mother. Although she has plenty she could confess to about the way she was not in Blake's life, and although Carver has not described *how* it is his fault, he has nonetheless confessed again. He realizes a moment later that he shouldn't confess to anyone else. He also realizes that he doesn't care. It would be hard for the DA to find Mitzi and he thinks that, based on her raggedy voice and her addictions, Mitzi might not be alive that much longer. Then he realizes that he would also be okay with the authorities finding out and punishing him. He says it would be a relief (p. 223).

After a goodbye to Nana Betsy, Blake returns home and his last thought about the goodbye day is that he feels the way he does after he has vomited. He doesn't really feel good, but he feels as though he has gotten rid of something that was making him feel really bad (p. 224).

CONFESSION DOESN'T SOLVE EVERYTHING

After the first goodbye day, there are several other occasions that act as foils for the confession he made to Nana Betsy. Each of these other occasions is very different from Nana Betsy's goodbye day. There is another meeting with his counselor, Dr. Mendez, in which Carver describes the entire goodbye day. Interestingly, when Carver tells Dr. Mendez about it, he realizes that he is confessing again, as completely as he did to his lawyer or Nana Betsy. But Mendez's response is not absolution but rather a focused analysis of Carver's emotions and how to respond to them rather than a consideration of his guilt (p. 227).

Later, the police detectives ask if they can interview Carver to hear his side of the story. Carver goes to the meeting with his parents and Mr. Krantz, his lawyer. The detectives ask a variety of questions: Was he aware at the time of the accident that his three friends were travelling in a car? Did he text Mars just before the accident? Was he aware that Mars was driving when he texted him? Who has he talked to about this accident? Is there anything he wishes he had done differently on August first (p. 243–44)?

And for each question they ask, Mr. Kranz responds for Carver the same way, saying that his client will take the fifth amendment and not answer the question. (p. 244). Essentially, Carver is being prevented (or protected) from confessing.

As well as the first goodbye day goes, that is how badly the second goodbye day goes. Eli's parents, Melissa and Pierce, who are going through a divorce, are looking for closure. Carver joins them for the day as does Jesmyn, Eli's girlfriend. While he is only friends with Jesmyn, Carver still feels guilty. Melissa and Pierce bring a jar of brightly colored sand with them to scatter at the base of a waterfall on one of Eli's favorite hikes. They take turns dropping sand into the water and saying something they loved about Eli. The ceremony, however, does not seem to do what they hoped it would. Carver confesses to the reader that every time it is his turn to scatter some sand, his mouth says something nice about Eli, but in his mind he is asking Eli for forgiveness (p. 283).

Unlike with Nana Betsy, Carver is not able to tell them how sorry he is. That is partly because of the tension between Melissa and Pierce and partly because the situation does not feel safe—especially after Pierce tells Carver that he had better not start dating Jesmyn. Since Carver is falling in love with Jesmyn, this is not easy for him to hear.

After that second goodbye day, Carver goes back to Dr. Mendez. During that session, Dr. Mendez asks Carver if he was able to confront anything that he had not confronted before. Carver's response is first to the reader, and then to Dr. Mendez. Carver thinks it is strange that he can confess murder to Dr. Mendez, but not the love he feels for Jesmyn. After a time, he is able to admit that he might be feeling something toward Jesmyn. Dr. Mendez responds that he suspects that has complicated matters. Carver tells Dr. Mendez that Eli's dad made it very clear that he didn't want Carver to date his dead son's girlfriend (p. 289–90).

Where Nana Betsy might be said to be aggressively forgiving, Pierce (and to a lesser extent Melissa) seem passive-aggressively clear that they will not forgive. They are deeply grieving and have no room for forgiveness right now. Carver summarizes it toward the end of his time with Dr. Mendez when he says that Eli's dad considers Carver responsible for the accident, but Carver doesn't want to accept that responsibility the way he did during his day with Nana Betsy (p. 300). But, of course, the importance of confessing is as much with the confessor as with the person being confessed to.

And Carver finds himself wanting to confess to Jesmyn how he feels about her. People speak sometimes of confessing their love for someone, and while this is a very different sort of confessing than admitting a crime, in Carver's case, there are similarities. When they go together to a concert, Carver finds himself thinking about how much he would like to kiss her. In that moment, he imagines Pierce, as a cartoon demon, at his shoulder telling him that he does not deserve this, that Jesmyn does not belong to him now and never will. Instead, the cartoon demon Pierce tells him that both of them belong to his dead son (p. 308).

After the concert, when Jesmyn is talking to the lead singer and getting a poster signed, Carver finds himself overcome by jealousy. Later he accuses Jesmyn of not honoring Eli when she is fawning over the musician. Then he confesses he has feelings for her. But, of course, it is too soon. After more words from Carver prompted by jealousy, the romance he had dreamed of has broken up before it had a chance to even exist. And it is his fault for confessing his love too soon. Another confession that did not go so well.

THE FINAL GOODBYE DAY: VENGEANCE OR FORGIVENESS

If Carver is shocked when the announcement comes that the investigation has found that he is not criminally responsible for the accident, he is more shocked when he gets a call from Judge Edwards, Mars's father, saying that he wants a goodbye day as well. If Nana Betsy offers forgiveness and Melissa and Pierce offer passive condemnation, Judge Edwards's goodbye day is one of punishment.

It starts with him taking Carver on a seven-mile run, a task so difficult that Carver ends up vomiting before he can finish. The Judge waits impatiently, then drives him to Mars's church where Carver listens uncomfortably while Judge Edwards preaches about justice. Then he brings Carver back to his home, gives him two trash bags, and tells him to clean Mars's room, and fill one bag with things that are to go to the Salvation Army, and the other bag with things to be thrown away. When Carver asks what he is supposed to do with things he thinks the Judge might want to see, the Judge barks out that everything either goes to the Salvation Army or gets thrown away.

As Carver sorts through his dead friend's room, he comes upon a comic that Mars illustrated that clearly was inspired by Mars's dad, which Carver thinks the Judge should see. But when he tries to give it to Judge Edwards, the Judge yells at him to shut up and calls him reckless and a murderer (p. 362). The judge then physically throws Carver out the door so that he tumbles onto the cement.

A few hours later, Judge Edwards is at Carver's door. He has read the comic and has realized that he didn't know his son at all, he only knew what he wanted him to be. He asks if Carver will tell him about his son. And then they have a real goodbye day—or at least part of one. Carver is able to tell the Judge some stories—and while he doesn't confess his crimes (it perhaps seems unnecessary since the Judge has seen the police report and knows the details of the crime), he does confess to the Judge how much he loved his friends, how much he misses them, and how much he is in grief for them.

Carver's final, full confession, comes when he has his last session with Dr. Mendez. Carver asks if he can tell the doctor a story. He proceeds to describe the accident in full detail, as he had done for his lawyer, but this time, the description turns into a combination of a story and a confession. Carver describes how this character in his story texts his friend who was driving, because he knew his friend would text back, then later finds out that all of them were killed when the car crashes. He explains that the character in the story is fairly certain that he caused the accident, but he isn't completely certain. The one thing he does know is that he didn't mean to hurt them and if he had known what was going to happen, he would never have taken the actions he did (p. 384).

There is, of course, more to the story. But that is the end of Carver's journey to confession. How do we get our students to not only see this theme clearly, but, through discussion, bring it out in the open on their own?

USING IGNATIAN IMAGERY TO DIG DEEPER INTO CARVER'S CONFESSION

Ignatian Imagery (sometimes called Ignatian Spirituality) is a reading discussion technique that relies on using your imaginary five senses to put yourself into a scene from the book. The teacher starts by choosing a passage from the book that both intersects with the theme being considered and offers enough imagery to activate their imaginations. With *Goodbye Days*, one passage that Bill has used with students is a section in chapter 9 that runs from page 65 to page 67. In this passage, Carver comes over to Nana Betsy's house several days after the funeral to help her weed her garden. Bill chose this passage because it has strong descriptions involving most of the senses.

The passage is also one of the first passages in the book that deals with confession. On page 67, after telling Nana Betsy the story of Blake improvising spaghetti with ketchup and mustard for sauce, the two of them laugh and wipe away tears. Carver thinks about how for a brief time he feels freed from guilt. It is like a tiny taste of being redeemed from his pain. And it tastes sweet (p. 67).

Before reading the passage aloud to their students, teachers should remind them to pay special attention to what the passage reveals about Carver's (and the author Jeff Zentner's) understanding and discovery of confession. In this case, the passage works extremely well because at no point in the passage does the word "confession" appear. This forces students to think beyond merely listening for the word, but instead imagine themselves into the story and its concepts. Teachers should also remind them to use all their senses to get a full picture of the narrative.

The teacher then reads the passage aloud. When the reading is finished, the teacher asks students if they would like to hear it a second time. Once students have done this exercise at least once, their answer is almost always yes. Teachers should pause between readings for them to have a moment to jot down their impressions.

After the teacher has read the passage, the teacher asks a couple of guiding questions to start the discussion:

1. From what point of view did you see the story from? (Though the story is told from Carver's point of view, some students see the scene from Nana Betsy's point of view, from the point of view of an overall storyteller, or sometimes from another point of view all together). What did that point of view allow you to see?
2. What in the passage connected you with the idea of confession? Students' responses to this question are often a surprise to the teacher.

Students might see, for example, connections between the description of Carver pulling weeds, and Carver trying to remove the undesirable thoughts and feelings from his mind by working for Nana Betsy, as if his actions are a kind of confession.

In one of Bill's classes, a student noted Carver's reluctance to come inside, drink the lemonade, and eat the sandwiches that Nana Betsy has made may be because he wants to keep punishing his body. Although this is not confession, it might be penance.

3. Did you notice anything during the reading that took your attention? This could be anything about the way it was told, how it was told, or what it was telling. Answers range widely, with students drawing connections and making observations far beyond the scope of our confession theme. But that richness often suggests ideas that we can bring back around to the theme.

For example, one student pointed out that Carver was so absorbed in his work that he didn't notice Nana Betsy returning from the store. The student mentioned that she really enjoyed when she could get lost in something, whether playing competitive volleyball or doing math problems. The class then speculated that perhaps all Carver wanted to do was forget. And that led to a discussion about the futility of trying to solve problems by trying to ignore or forget them.

Ignatian Imagery allows students to dig more deeply into the stories they read. Instead of limiting their interactions to a chapter-by-chapter reading with weekly reading quizzes, and a discussion at the end of the book about what the themes were and whether students liked the book, the class can consider the entire book as a prayer, offered by the author, that considers the idea of confession from multiple facets. Teachers can then use Ignatian Spirituality to connect students more deeply with the noveland help them relate the novel to their own lives.

Goodbye Days offers students a rich and robust experience following the theme of confession across multiple characters both analytically and, as we see with Ignatian Imagery, also emotionally, with their senses, and in terms of point of view. Other discussion approaches in this book can unlock other aspects of *Goodbye Days*.

Chapter 5

Seeing Equanimity in *brown girl dreaming*
Using Havruta

One of the poems that comprise *brown girl dreaming* evokes a peaceful comfort with the world. That poem, titled "Home," describes the moment that the main character's mother is welcomed back into her parent's home, the warmth of her grandparent's embrace, the tears wiped from her mother's face, and the way she, as a newly-born infant, was nestled deep in all this love.

In this short stanza there is acceptance, healing, enfolding, and a love you can sit inside of. And amidst the injustice of the world, the discord between people, the difficulty of separation, there is also a peace, a settled feeling within that moment, and a freedom from needing to be somewhere else, doing something else, or worrying about something else. There is an equanimity.

brown girl dreaming is a Newbery Honor book, a National Book Award winner, and Coretta Scott King Award winner. Woodson has written many other young adult books including *Red at the Bone* (2019), *Another Brooklyn* (2016), and *Miracle's Boys* (2000).

Reading *brown girl dreaming* is a sensual experience, by which we mean it involves all of the senses. We recommend that readers buy the original hardback version of the text with thick and musky paper, glue smell, and artistic cover of a young girl silhouetted in the twilight as the sky changes from blue to gold.

In the book Jacqueline Woodson explores how she became a writer while traversing the places of her childhood with an abundance of love for all who loved her. Love is infused throughout her story, even as she recounts the suffering of an African-American family in the 1960's and 1970's during the height of the Civil Rights Movement. In order to distinguish between Jaqueline Woodson the author and Jacqueline the character, we will refer to the author of the book as Woodson and the character within the book as Jacqueline.

Helping students to see a young adult novel as a prayer that the author is offering to readers, to God, or to the universe is also a way for students to learn new concepts in a way that exercises their ability to dig deeper and understand further. The word *equanimity* may be new to some readers, or familiar but not clearly defined. It is a term both important to spiritual growth and personal well-being for many traditions, especially those that originated in the East, but it is also hard to define. This partly because the term is a synthesis of many concepts that have emerged from mindfulness practices.

In this chapter we will learn what equanimity is, see how Jacqueline Woodson addresses equanimity in *brown girl dreaming,* and introduce how we can use the ancient practice of havruta to lead students in reading and discussing the book and in understanding and reflecting on equanimity as Woodson's family navigates the effects of racism.

SUMMARY OF *BROWN GIRL DREAMING*

In *brown girl dreaming* (notice the convention of breaking the rules of capitalization), Woodson outlines her family tree on both her father's and her mother's side. The Woodson clan considers itself as a member of American royalty through Sally Hemmings, Jefferson's slave-mistress. The family is talented, loving, and proud of their roots.

As a child, Jacqueline develops a great love for the writing of Langston Hughes and showcases his verse while trying on aspects of his style in the text. The book starts chronologically at Jacqueline's birth in 1963 in Columbus, Ohio, in a country she describes as being caught in the tension between Black People and White people (p. 1), She recounts that her father's family was one of the only Black families in the town of Nelsonville, Ohio. As Woodson describes the tastes and textures of her early childhood, readers read between the lines and see her parents' relationships unraveling.

The artistic enjambment of poetry and spare selection of words create the white space which runs throughout the book. Chapters can be read quickly because white space adds to the beauty of each page and causes places for the eye to rest and the brain to think.

The second part of the book is told in South Carolina as Jacqueline and her siblings move in with her maternal grandparents, the very loving Irbys. Her devout grandmother is a Jehovah's Witness. Her grandfather is more spiritual than religious as he works the land and believes in the earth and the coolness of the soil (p. 48). The South is still segregated but the Irbys hold fast to Black pride; good, homemade food; Grandma's Bible reading; and grandfather

Gunnar's loving ways. Jacqueline's sister Odella models a love of reading and Jacqueline hungers to write, starting with the magical shape of a J, the first letter of her name. Her brother, Hope, finds comfort in the superhero comics Gunnar brings home to him.

They are taught to speak crisply and clearly and are warned not to ever call anyone "Ma'am," As the South wages a war of segregation, Jacqueline is paying attention to both the ugliness of racism and to the beauty of life in the South, including the taste of lemon chiffon ice cream on her tongue, and admiration of the people, both Black and White, who are fighting a war of justice. As her mother leaves for New York alone, Grandpa becomes sicker, and Jacqueline notices that her grandmother's faith seems to be based on fear even as Jacqueline becomes more active in her own faith. Finally, her mother returns to her with a new baby brother in tow.

Part three of the book is about Jacqueline's childhood in Brooklyn. At first it is a place of despondency for Jacqueline, but then she meets more members of her extended family. She talks of meeting people from Greenville, Spartanburg, and Charleston who all talked like her grandparents did and ate what her grandparents ate (p. 145) and Brooklyn becomes home. Jacqueline falls in love with writing through sniffing the paper of her composition notebook, then writing her full name: Jacqueline Amanda Woodson, and loving her kind first grade teacher, Ms. Friedler, who greets her at the door every morning.

Jacqueline continues to practice her Jehovah's Witness faith, but her mother is not interested in the faith, and Jacqueline wishes she too could say the pledge of allegiance with her classmates and have holidays too, things that are forbidden in her grandmother's faith.

Jacqueline realizes in Brooklyn that her sister is gifted, but she is not—but she also learns she is driven to tell stories and then visits Greenville again for the summer when her new baby brother, Roman, gets sick from eating lead paint. There are moments of equanimity in the strife where all is well in spite of the pain. In a poem called "the johnny pump," Woodson describes a piece of joy on a hot, dirty street. She sees her mother, who never goes outside without shoes in the city, remove her sandals, stand at the edge of the curb, and let the water from an open fire hydrant cool her bare feet. In that moment, Jacqueline notices her mother is gazing up at the sky visible between the buildings and breaking into a big smile. (p. 147).

Part four describes Jacqueline and her siblings returning home to Brooklyn. Roman, her baby brother, comes home from the hospital. Jacqueline makes a best friend, Maria, and learns about the music of poetry in school and reads a book called *Stevie* over and over, delighting in the fact that Stevie looks like her and Stevie's story is filled with pictures of brown people. She tells her family she wants to be a writer and writes her first book about butterflies, which consists of seven poems, mostly haikus. Her uncle is sent to prison and beloved Grandfather dies.

Part five recounts how Jacqueline's grandmother moves to Brooklyn, plants a Mimosa tree, and how the baby tree grows through the Brooklyn snow, surviving against all odds, a miracle. Jacqueline realizes how much she is like her late grandfather and feels good about herself as her general spirituality overtakes a particular religion. She continues to tell made up stories to entertain her classmates. She asks her mother what she believes in. Her mother responds that she believes in God, the resurrection Brooklyn, and the four other members of her family. Jacqueline learns that Bushwick was started by the Dutch and former slaves who bought their freedom. This gives her hope.

Then she finds more knowledge when her uncle is released from jail and becomes Robert the Muslim and tells Jacqueline many new stories. While Jacqueline learns about Angela Davis and the Black Panthers, all the white people move out of her neighborhood. Ms. Vivo, her teacher, lets her know she is a writer and teaches her about feminism. Jacqueline writes poetry about Martin with his heart of gold and she dreams of becoming a writer and remembers how once she only knew the letter J.

In the penultimate chapter, she writes her creed. This is the section we will use to consider how havruta might be used to open up discussion of Woodson's writing, particularly how it contains many moments of equanimity as juxtaposition to a troubled time in history.

The book concludes with photographs of Woodson's family, letting readers know that Woodson is more than the narrative's protagonist, Jacqueline. She is a living, breathing woman who learned as a child to live with equanimity in racist times: Readers see photographs of Jacqueline as a child, Jacqueline's parents, Jacqueline's siblings, the Woodsons of Ohio, the Irbys of South Carolina. It's lovely to see these faces and realize that all the beautiful characters are or were real people who actually lived and learned and became intricately involved in the stories that Jacqueline has written.

WHAT IS EQUANIMITY?

Bussing, Osterman, and Mathiessen define spirituality as "humans' search for meaning in life," while arguing that religion, in contrast, "involves an organized entity with rituals and practices about a higher power or God" (2006, p. 270). Spiritual growth often occurs in silence and isolation from other humans, especially when one is going through traumatic events that others may not be able to relate to (Bussing, Osterman, & Matthiessen, p. 268). Equanimity does not function separately from other attributes of spirituality, but in conjunction with prayer, trust in a higher being, insight, awareness, wisdom, transcendence, and conviction.

Equanimity is one of the "Four Immeasurables" in Buddhism that develops compassion and alleviates mental suffering (Weber, 2019). Weber suggests considering defining equanimity as "Present moment open awareness and conviction in nonreaction towards our own discrimination faculties (pleasure, displeasure or neutrality) so we can respond with care and compassion" (in *The Psychologist*, letters). Mason (2016) compares equanimity to grace in the Christian tradition as portrayed in Barthes' *Morning Diary*, personal writing that Barthes penned while grieving the loss of his wife.

As Mason explains, "The dynamic influence of the divine experienced by the believer through faith, grace has the *logos* to meditation or prayer. For the grieving Barthes, grace promises relief without negating the course of bereavement and so enables the act of writing" (p. 327–343). When grace occurs, the suffering individual realizes they are not alone but part of a divine body. Grace is predicated on suffering and relieves suffering (p. 328). When grace is realized, conversion happens in the Christian tradition, when "God 'puts' religion 'into the heart'" and faith becomes personal and relational with God (Mason, 2016, p. 332).

Equanimity, in the Buddhist tradition, is part of wisdom, the path to enlightenment. The ultimate purpose of Buddhism is to obtain enlightenment and to share ways of enlightenment with others. To obtain enlightenment, one must recognize the significance of emptiness and the significance of equanimity. Mahayana Buddhism describes six stages of perfection comprised of six virtues: generosity, morality, patience, diligence, meditation, and wisdom, the most important virtue that includes all the other virtues (Mann, p. 302). To recognize the significance of emptiness and equanimity is to find Wisdom.

As Mann explains, "The practice of relieving suffering requires that one empties oneself from preconceptions and personal desires so as to be receptive to living in the moment as it comes, accepting the moment with no attachment to prior ideas" (p. 303). If one is to relieve the suffering of others, one must approach them with empathy and offer an emptiness that "renounces his or her personal narcissistic needs" (p. 303). This allows those on the path to Wisdom to offer empathy without judgement to others. Equanimity allows this emptiness because it exists without judgement for any person; whatever happens to oneself and to others can be faced (p. 306).

Not judging other people allows wisdom to flourish because equanimity is "learning to accept loss and gain, good-repute and ill-repute, praise and censure, sorrow and happiness, all with detachment, equally, for oneself and for others. It is a tranquil state of mind—not being overpowered by delusions, mental distress or agitation" (Mann, p. 302). When equanimity is present in a person, that person is open and accepting and not led by impermanent emotions.

The Buddha describes the state of equanimity as follows: "When seeing a form with the eye . . . When hearing a sound with ear . . . When smelling an aroma with the nose . . . When tasting a flavor with the tongue . . . When touching a tactile sensation with the body . . . When cognizing an idea with the intellect, there arises in him what is agreeable, what is disagreeable, what is agreeable and disagreeable . . . If he wants—in the presence of what is loathsome and what is not—cutting himself off from both, he remains in equanimity, alert, and mindful" (Weber, 2021, p.152).

The idea of equanimity as withholding judgement is present in Jesus's repeated admonitions for his followers to not judge or to stop judging. Equanimity has been described as "nonjudgement" or "decentering" (Weber, p. 151) and has been described "as the most significant psychological element in the improvement of well-being" (Cited in Weber, p. 152; Desbordes, et al. 2015). Farb et al. describe equanimity as "the suspension of judging experience to be intrinsically good or bad" (2012, p. 71). The point of suspending initial judgment is so that a deeper insight for judgment may emerge.

Equanimity also seems to support prosocial change and an increased sense of mental well-being by bringing about emotional regulation (p. 152). Traumatized Cambodian monks found that equanimity helped regulate anger (Nickerson and Hinton, p. 156).

A study focusing on equanimity as "learning to care for strangers" featured at-risk adolescents who had been traumatized (Reddy, et al., 2013). This study found that the older an adolescent female became, the less compassion she had toward herself. As self-compassion decreased, so depression increased. When adolescents developed equanimity through present-centered awareness, they became more compassionate towards self. Nickerson and Hinton (2011) observed equanimity helps with anger regulation because it creates distance from self in the middle of an event, allowing adolescents to grow in compassion.

Practicing embodied awareness brings back the intentionality necessary for equanimity (McCulloch, p. 86). This means that a leader desperately needing to find clarity in a stressful situation can find means to be present to rest in the uncertainty of the demands of leadership (p. 86). "When one is fully present, it is as if one radiates a panacea for challenging times, creating and holding an expanded moment, allowing for different options to emerge" (p. 86). It requires listening to one's body before listening without premature judgement to the points of views of others tangled in complex situations.

EQUANIMITY AND CARITAS IN
BROWN GIRL DREAMING

Sometimes this listening can take place in the act of writing. Woodson's *brown girl dreaming* contains ten haiku poems on "how to listen." Haikus rely on syllables which rely on breath. In the tenth and final haiku on how to listen, Woodson writes that she needs to write about what she thinks she knows, secure in the knowledge that the knowing for certain will come as she writes. She just needs to keep listening for it. Living in the moment means trusting that the knowing will come as one continues to listen. This is the faith that has also been called equanimity.

Equanimity starts with self-love and self-care but then extends to the care of others. Watson's Philosophy and Science of Caring introduces the construct of Caritas which is a precursor to developing equanimity. Caritas means first "learn[ing] how to offer caring, love, forgiveness, compassion, and mercy to ourselves before we can offer equanimity, gentleness, and dignity before we can accept, respect, and care for others within a professional caring-healing model" and also "treat[ing] ourselves with loving-kindness and equanimity, gentleness, and dignity before we can accept, respect, and care for others within a professional caring-healing model" (p. 1694).

Linton and Koonmen describe how Caritas can be developed in a helping profession (nursing) by implementing eight practices to reduce stress and build others up. Jacqueline Woodson, though a child, participates in these practices as she learns to love herself and her family.

First, equanimity cannot function in stress. However, developing close relationships with those around us reduces stress. Opening dialogue through one-on-one conversations and through developing relationships beyond obligations at work or in a family is an excellent first step.

Woodson's poetry uses the dialogue of her family to illustrate how, by listening to her relatives, Jacqueline grows to appreciate the differences in their unique gifts. In a poetic chapter entitled "gunnar's children," she describes her maternal grandfather as appearing to her to be the tallest person in their town. She also sees him as the most handsome. She describe his angular face and lightly-colored eyes, hands willed with warmth and strength, and how he reminds them that they are his children (p. 51). Equanimity realizes how important each person is when one knows one's self. Especially after Gunnar's death, Jacqueline realizes Gunnar has become a part of her and a reason she notices and listens to others as he did.

The second practice of building equanimity through developing Caritas or self-care involves practicing mindfulness through awareness of thoughts, practicing presence, and breathing techniques to destress. Woodson does this as she writes, especially her haikus on how to listen. In her "how to listen #6," Woodson describes how Jacqueline accomplishes mindfulness by sitting in a particular spot, in the shadow of a particular oak tree when the rest of the world can fade away (p. 225). In this instance, Jacqueline is developing presence by allowing nature to consume her thoughts.

A third practice requires cultivating spiritual practices which differ by individual but often include prayer and meditating on a sacred text as a form of self-care. The faith of Grandma Irby does not work for a young Jacqueline because it consists mostly of saying no to things. As she describes in the poem "because we're witnesses," Grandma Irby says no to Halloween, Christmas, and birthdays even though the other students laugh when Jacqueline and her siblings have to leave the room just as the birthday child starts to distribute chocolate cupcakes. Jacqueline and her siblings have to pretend they don't want to touch each sprinkle on the cupcakes and eat them one by one (p. 164).

The fourth step in creating self-care and developing equanimity is strengthening a healthy self-relationship by disrupting negative thoughts when they emerge and creating new paths of thinking in the brain which affects the rest of the body. In the final lines of "what I believe," Jacqueline proclaims her new religion based on yes (p. 318). She does this because she realizes her faith goes beyond the rules she learned as a Jehovah's Witness to include new ways of thinking other family members taught her, including resting in not knowing all the answers and being able to remain in the present.

The fifth process invites expressing negative feelings by listening to stories of self and others. After many stories of injustice and inequity, a moment of reprieve comes in the poem about the fabric store owned by a white woman. The following lines from that poem describe a proprietor who acts as humans should. The owner of the store pulls out rolls of fabric so that Jacqueline's grandmother can feel the texture. The owner and Grandmother talk about how the fabric drapes and which way the nap runs and good places to cinch he waist for a child's skirt. Jacqueline concludes that in that store her grandmother is not Colored or Negro. They are not potential thieves or something to be ashamed of. At that store, they are seen as people. (p. 91). This juxtaposition of hope in the midst of violence allows Jacqueline to express pain and sorrow and glimpse a more just world, even if only in the fabric store.

A sixth process is proactive as an individual creates healing environments by creating caring spaces with appropriate lighting, noise levels, and reducing atmospheric pollutants that add stressors to our bodies. Although Woodson does not keep house with a focus on creating serenity, she does create a place in the world that she can love, where she can belong, and where she can love words.

In the poem, "the earth from far away," Woodson explains how being part of the world starts with her journey of literacy, including understanding that her name begins with the letter J. (p. 316). By listening and recalling how her older sister taught her how to write helps Woodson create a loving place in her mind.

The seventh step to developing Caritas is taking time off for restoration and refreshment in times of intense stress. In "how to listen #9" Woodson writes about a place under the back porch when she can write without anyone bothering her (p. 299). Getting away from it all in the middle of chaos is necessary to develop self-care that can develop into equanimity.

The final step to developing self-care is opening up to miracles, "an event that causes wonder and is in some way unusual or contrary to expectations" (Koonmen, p. 1700). Woodson discovers such a miracle in the poem "each world." She has come to understand that every day there is a new wold that she can become part of. That includes the worlds of the different places she has lived, the different people he had lived with, the different faith traditions she has been raised in, and somehow they all are gathered together into the person that she is (p. 320). This is the miracle of *You* which Woodson realizes is the culmination of all the stories and the people and the love she has written down and treasured in her heart.

THE HISTORY OF HAVRUTA

Zoltan and Ter Kuile (2020) explain havruta in this way: "Havruta is a several hundred-year-old practice where two people are reading a book together, usually it's the *Talmud*, and the idea is that two people together can learn everything that they need to learn if they are willing to have an open and rigorous discussion amongst themselves and with the book."

While havruta can also work on a whole class level, it is effective in partner-pairs. This chapter will describe havruta for two people. One person poses a question, then poses a potential response to that question. The second person then responds to the same question. Their objective is not to find the one correct response, but to work toward a deeper understanding through the aggregate of their responses. It is remarkable how far such a conversation can go and how much the text gives to the readers as well as how much the readers bring to the text.

On the website *My Jewish Learning*, Rachel Gelfman Schultz describes more about the history of havruta (https://www.myjewishlearning.com/article/havruta-learning-in-pairs/). Schultz observes that the word "havruta" means "fellowship," and that the study of the Torah is meant to be social. Havruta depends on pairs who " . . . struggle to understand the meaning of each passage and discusses how to apply it to the larger issues and even to their own lives" (Gelfman Schultz, https://www.myjewishlearning.com/article/havruta-learning-in-pairs/).

Havruta is learned in *beit midrash* (a study hall) where a roomful of scholars debate important literary passages, synthesize those meanings somehow, and come to new insights. The ideology of havruta comes from the *Talmud* which observes, "Two scholars sharpen one another." A sixteenth century commentator of rabbinical traditions, Ovadiah Seforno interprets Ecclesiastes 4:10 to mean, "Two are better than one, in that they derive greater benefit from their efforts. For if they should fall, the one will raise up the other, as opposed to if one falls when there is no one to raise him."

A fifteenth century Spanish commentator, Don Yitzak Abravanel encouraged Jews to, "Make for yourself a rabbi and acquire for yourself a friend" (Mishnah Avot 1.6). Before going to the rabbi to discuss important topics in a sacred text, one was to discuss these thoughts first with a friend who would also investigate the truth of that passage and add depth to the meaning of the words.

Initially, havruta was considered a kind of tutoring strategy for weaker students of sacred Jewish texts. In the early twentieth century this changed when after World War 1, the Yeshwot opened doors to all Jewish men and not just to elite scholars. Then havruta became commonplace because anyone could be scholars of the sacred texts.

SUMMARY OF TEXT SELECTION OF *BROWN GIRL DREAMING* FOR HAVRUTA

In the penultimate chapter of *brown girl dreaming*, Jacqueline Woodson writes a chapter entitled "what I believe." In this poetic chapter, every line is an expression of equanimity Woodson has learned through experiences that have traversed places, people, and ideas. The poem is a series of lists and starkly contrasting "ands," each line starting with the words "I believe." She believes in God and evolution, the Bible and the Qur'an, in Christmas and the New World, that everyone has good in them despite belief differences. She believes in the South and in Black and White and riding a bus and refusing to ride a bus. She also believes in Brooklyn, writing and listening, good words and bad words. She concludes this poem with lines that state that she believes in the possibilities of days to come and also believes in the potential and experience of the present moment (p. 319).

We selected this passage because it seemed to us that it contained potential for discussion and also touched on the theme we wanted to focus on, the idea of the book as a prayer for equanimity.

PRACTICING HAVRUTA FEATURING EQUANIMITY WITH "WHAT I BELIEVE"

Earlier in the book we wrote about ways that these sacred text reading techniques can be modified for use with smaller groups or the entire class. Later we will describe a way to use havruta with an entire class. However using havruta to get at equanimity offers some particular challenges. In this case, before students can engage in finding how a through-line of a search for equanimity runs through *brown girl dreaming*, the teacher will need to make sure that the students understand the concept and know what they are looking for. This will require more structured supports along the way.

This next section will describe how Kris and Bill model those structures. In her classes, Kris uses large Post-It notes with attributes of equanimity pulled from earlier definitions in the chapter. Kris begins by filling out a large Post-It note with several definitions of equanimity: (1) It is present moment open awareness, (2) It is nonreaction or lack of judging, (3) It is grace that offers relief without negating bereavement by allowing the grievant to be part of a divine body, (4) it is predicated on suffering and relieves suffering, (5) it has been called emptiness of oneself and freedom from narcissism, (6) it has been considered emotional regulation.

As we read Woodson's "what I believe" together (p. 318), we attempt to attach the best definitions to the first stanza:

> Kris: Based on this poem, what is equanimity? As I look at the first lines, I really see definition two: the lack of judging aspect of equanimity. It seems like this allows Woodson to add "ands" to what might be thought of as binaries that don't need to be binaries if you are suspending judgement. I mean, many Christian believers in God who have been trained in science also believe in evolution, for example.

> Bill: Good point, and I also see evidence of definition number four: "It is predicated on suffering and relieves suffering." I see that in the lines about her mother and he community refusing to ride segregated buses. That evokes the history of the Civil Rights Movement and the struggle for dignity and freedom from injustice and suffering.

> Kris: I also see this poem as a love story to her relatives' belief systems. Jacqueline accepts and loves her family so much and wants to keep them around the table, especially given how much loss they have already experienced. I would consider that freedom from narcissism, definition number five. In this poem she alludes to her grandmother's Jehovah Witness faith by mentioning God and the Bible, but she also believes in her grandfather's spiritual connection with earth and kindness to his loved ones—sort of a relief from the dogmatism and the good works of her grandmother.

Bill: Yes, and I also see emotional regulation from definition five. I see it in reference to nonjealousy towards her sister, but also her self-compassion in enjoying too-easy books. It takes emotional regulation to know when to ride a bus and when not to ride a bus. Rosa Parks certainly sacrificed, as did many others during the Montgomery boycott by not riding the bus. I guess I also see definition number four in reference to the bus boycotts in the line about how sometimes it is necessary to suffer in order to relieve suffering.

Kris: Right. And I think there are more examples of equanimity if we read on. The line with all the terms that are easy to see as binaries. Malcolm X and Martin Luther King had very different ways of seeking justice and are often thought of as opposites—almost like you have to chose one or the other. Woodson's equanimity allows her to embrace both.

The phrase that mentions buckeyes and Birmingham refers to her decision to embrace her life in Ohio and her life in Alabama, even though they are very different, just as she sees writing and listening as two distinct parts of herself one part shy and polite while the other part has a voice she heeds to raise, and needs to use the words to say what she has to say, even if those words are considered impolite. And when she says she believes in Brooklyn, isn't she embracing a place of different cultures, people, walks of life, and diversity, all rolled up in one brash, unapologetic passage?

Bill: I couldn't have said it better. I can see it now. In a world that is always trying to put her in a box and make her judge between different aspects of who she is and how she will relate to other people, Jacqueline is deciding not to decide—to embrace opposites and sometimes contradictory lives and suspend the need to accept or condemn. She is putting this all together as a kind of grace.

Kris: The last stanza is only two lines that really seem like definition one, present moment awareness. It is an echo of what her mother said, about how she believes in right now.

Bill: It is also nonjudgement of those who believe in the heaven of some future point in time and those who can only believe in the present. I mean that covers a lot of ways of believing.

Kris: I wonder if we can apply the principles of Caritas to how Jacqueline incorporates equanimity into her belief system.

So we fill out another giant Post-It note: How to develop Caritas for Equanimity: (1) develop relationships, (2) create mindfulness and awareness of thoughts in the present by figuring out techniques to destress, (3) sustain spiritual practices like prayer, (4) disrupt thoughts and develop new, more positive thinking, (5) allow negative feelings to be expressed by listening to stories and telling your own story, (6) create healing spaces for others, (7) allow yourself to be refreshed, (8) open up to miracles.

Bill: Maybe it works to think of this poem as Woodson's relationships coming together to help her form a more authentic belief system. And the very act of writing about what she believes allows her to be mindful of what she believes and thinks.

Kris: The act of reading and writing can play therapeutic roles in allowing people to destress by reading or writing to "know we are not alone"—a quote often attributed to C.S. Lewis.

Bill: Plus, we know that reading young adult literature can be a spiritual or even a religious practice if we apply strategies to meditate on sacred texts and discover new things.

Kris: Which could allow us to disrupt former ways of thinking and renew our minds. This is an especially pure book about a child who loves so many people and falls in love with language, especially poetry. Woodson writes several haikus about listening that compose an entire chapter. I think listening could be regarded as a spiritual practice if we allow others to show themselves as image-bearers of God even in their most distressing stories. That takes developing deep relationships to have that kind of deep talk, though.

Bill: And that is a big part of equanimity, right? I think relationships only happen when you can see beyond the façade people present. Sometimes listening to stories allows us to express negative feelings. And these negative feelings need to be noticed, and named, and, especially in times of trauma, need to be told to gather and build compassion and understanding.

Kris: I think allowing all kinds of stories can create healing spaces for everyone to tell their story and not be misunderstood which so often happens when deep relationships are not deeply formed and people share what they believe and feel judged by others who might not understand their point of view. Plus it can be stressful to tell a story of trauma.

Bill: Yeah, and the thing about books is we develop deep relationships with characters and we can learn to understand and sympathize without harming the relationship. For example, I like how Jacqueline refrains from judgment as she moves away from the traditional religion of her grandmother and its focus on hell and realizes that her grandfather also has contributed to her belief system with his caring ways. Ultimately Jacqueline believes that her country needs a lot of work but there are many reasons to care about the people in the world and find beauty in it.

Kris: I think perfection is a miracle. We recognize it so rarely, but it should slow us down, and we should take it in. Believing in the perfect moment of now seems like Woodson is open to miracles. That's a pretty positive place to end.

Havruta allowed Kris and Bill to pursue application of a concept, equanimity, that is difficult to understand. Havruta enables close reading of Woodson's poetry and allows students to provide textual evidence to buttress a claim. The practice also encourages integration of history in order to understand the allusions to historical people and events within the novel.

Havruta can help students out of shallow or binary thinking to the more complex thinking of equanimity. Bill and Kris observed the importance of writing to Jacqueline so that she can articulate an authentic belief system rich in equanimity which requires listening which necessitates suspending judgement to do it well. They were also able to notice examples of beautiful language including alliteration and repetition. Telling stories often helps people get to the truth which is the point, on some level, of all literature

It may be helpful for teachers to allow havruta to be open-ended but also introduce structure by providing students with some general talking points. In this case, Bill and Kris use definitions of equanimity and how to develop Caritas as some structure. The structure does not dictate the direction of the conversation or the ultimate conclusions that can be reached as havruta is meant to construct knowledge of a complex text together in a kind of literary fellowship where partners build on each other's previous responses and can create a world of meaning from a text.

Seeing *brown girl dreaming* as a prayer of equanimity and using havruta as a way to anchor that understanding with the text of the book provides a richer and fuller experience for all of your students.

Chapter 6

Thankfulness in *The War That Saved My Life*

When people think about prayers of thankfulness, they might picture a stereotypical scene with a small child reciting a laundry list of material possessions they are thankful for. When we talk of a YA book as a prayer of thankfulness, though, it is more about a character (and often a community of characters) moving from a position of self-centeredness (and often pain) to a position of thankfulness that reaches beyond being glad someone gave you a toy or material object, to an appreciation for life and the world that transcends human relationships.

The War That Saved My Life by Kimberly Brubaker Bradley (2015) won a Newbery Honor Award in 2016. The main character in the book is younger than usual in a young adult book (11 to 12 years old), but the book has a large readership among both middle school and high school readers. And the depth and maturity of the themes in the book (abuse, grief, oppression of those involved in same-sex relationships, developing autonomy and agency, and the horrors of war) seem suited to this older audience than to the age of the protagonist.

Bradley has written a sequel titled *The War I Finally Won* (2018) and several other young adult books, including *Fighting Words* (2019).

In this chapter we consider how *The War That Saved My Life* can be read as a prayer of thankfulness. We could just as easily consider it as a prayer of anger, a prayer of lament, a prayer of yearning, a prayer of pilgrimage, a prayer of reconciliation, and perhaps others. Each of these readings would yield different insights into how two characters, Ada and Susan, grow in their connections to something beyond themselves. Thankfulness seems most appropriate, though, as the story movement toward thankfulness is complicated, arduous, and truthful.

Like the guttural prayers mentioned by Larsen in his book (and explained in our introduction), the movement of the story toward thankfulness is halting, full of backward movement, and not fully realized. Sometimes in contemporary society, we think of prayers as requests that are answered in a positive way (or, if they aren't answered positively, they are at best a waste of time, at worst a proof against the existence of God), but many holy books describe prayer as a calling out, a struggle, and a wrestling with God. The book of Psalms, read by Jewish and Christian worshipers alike, is filled with prayers of anguish, of asking why, and sometimes even of despair.

Students may argue rightly that although *The War That Saved My Life* ends hopefully, none of the characters progresses to an end state where they are indisputably able to live a life filled with thankfulness. At the end of the story, the main character still has a club foot and although she and her brother seem to have escaped Mam for good, the house they have come to consider home has just burned down. They are still struggling.

One of the differences in the characters is that they have learned to reflect on the world around them and sometimes, to be thankful for the good things there are. We will trace how thankfulness develops in several characters in the novel. This book is rich in what it offers for discussion about thankfulness.

ADA: LIVING A LIFE WITH NOTHING TO BE THANKFUL FOR

The War That Saved My Life is a historical fiction novel set in England during World War II. We meet Ada, born with a foot twisted upside-down, which makes it nearly impossible for her to put any weight on it, or for her to learn to walk. Her mother, whom Ada calls Mam, is a single woman living in poverty in London. Mam is so embarrassed by Ada and is so full of anger toward her that she heaps Ada with verbal abuse, tells her she is worthless, beats her daily, underfeeds her, forbids her from ever leaving the tiny flat, and sometimes locks her in a roach-infested cupboard. Ada takes the abuse in an effort to protect her younger brother, Jamie.

Ada's life seems to offer almost nothing to be thankful for, but when her mother is gone, Ada sometimes looks out the window and waves at people in her neighborhood, though her mother has forbidden such activity. She isn't exactly thankful for the window, but it does give her hope.

Ada's character at the outset of the book, then, is not only living in a situation in which she has little to be thankful for, but more importantly, she has been told she is worthless for so long, her psyche is not intact enough to recognize any aspect of life as a gift—because she doesn't view herself as worthy of gifts.

And yet, something in her manages to hope. She has been trying to learn to walk on her foot, practicing in secret while her mother is working, and wiping up the blood from her blisters before her mom gets home. Her younger brother Jamie is allowed to go outside, and he becomes Ada's window to the world. When Jamie finds out that the children of London are going to be evacuated so they can be safe from German bombing, Ada hatches a plan and soon they are fleeing the flat while their mother is asleep, and though Ada is in pain at every step, they make it to the train station and are soon on their way out of London.

On the train, watching the landscape blur past, Ada admits that most of the other evacuating children were not happy to be leaving like she was (p. 24). There is momentary relief there, but Ada is afraid of her past catching up with her and fearful of what the coming arrival in the country holds as well. Perhaps it will be worse than what she leaves behind.

When they arrive in the countryside, Ada and Jamie line up with the other children, and families come by, picking up the children they have been assigned. One by one every other child is picked by a family until finally only Ada and Jamie stand, dirty, smelly, and unwanted, on the station platform.

While their environment has changed from a cramped and uncomfortable flat in an area of London that is economically disadvantaged, to a beautiful countryside with ponies and green fields, their status remains the same. Ada and Jamie are unwanted, and in that state, there is no room in them to be thankful for anything.

They meet a stern woman with a clipboard (whom Ada and Jamie will later come to know as Lady Thornton). She is in charge of housing the evacuees and tells them not to worry, that she has the perfect place for them. They can stay with a single lady, who Lady Thornton says is very nice. Jamie shakes his head at that and says that his Mam told him that nice people wouldn't want to have Jamie and Ada live with them, The clipboard woman tells him that the woman they will be staying with isn't *really* that nice (p. 33).

MEETING SUSAN, WHO IS NOT READY TO LOVE ANYONE

Any good YA book, in fact, any good piece of literature at all, explores ideas and themes across multiple characters and situations. If Ada and Jamie are unable to experience thankfulness because of the horror they have fled, the woman who takes them in, Susan, is unable to experience thankfulness because of the grief she still suffers from. As the story unfolds we see both stories move toward thankfulness in very different ways.

Ada initially describes Susan as being pale and thin and dressed in black (p. 36). In their first conversation with Jamie and Ada, she admits that she doesn't know anything about caring for children. Ada reflects that she has never needed to be taken care of, but decides not to tell Susan that (p. 38).

Schat (2020) conducted extensive interviews with thirteen young adults about their experiences in grades 6 to 12 that focused on the relationship of caring between students and teachers. Schat found that while some educational research describes a loss or lack of care in our educational systems, the problem is not that teachers do not care for their students, but that, as he puts it:

> The problem can be better described as a disconnect between teacher caring and intentions and the perceptions and experiences of far too many of their students.... Too often, intended care fails to translate into experienced care. Most teachers are caring and believe that they are communicating care successfully. But some of their students do not experience the care the teacher offers. (Schat, 2020, p. 22)

Schat argues that in order for people to care for each other, they must both recognize that what is intended as care is, in fact, care.

In *The War That Saved My Life*, though the children have escaped their toxic environment, and though they are now in a situation where they are cared for, safe, well-fed, warm, clothed, and free of abuse, they cannot see that care as care yet. And this obstacle to understanding care is two-sided. Ada and Jamie have been neglected for so long, they feel like they do not need love. And we soon learn that Susan is mourning in isolation the death of Becky, her best friend and lover.

Because of this, when Susan engages in caring actions (bathing, feeding, clothing, and talking to the children), she seems to do so in a daze. Ada describes her as cross, sharp, and not nice. Susan is providing the first real care the children have ever had, but neither she nor the children are in a position to understand that it is care.

In Ada's case, she is unable to trust anyone other than Jamie. When Susan takes her to a doctor and tells her that her foot can be fixed by surgery, Ada thinks Jamie is foolish for believing it. Ada feels nervous in the shops because they have so much nice stuff in them (p. 52). Later, Ada thinks about how filled with softness and goodness Susan's place seems and yet how it also frightens her. Ada seems unable to accept that she is worthy of her new reality.

Susan struggles with bouts of deep depression over the death of Becky. There are days when she never leaves her bed, or sits and stares into space, unable to do more than feed the children. If Ada is unable to accept a new reality, Susan is unable to leave her old reality. And she heaps guilt upon grief. After spending the better part of a day in bed, Susan tells the children that she thinks she has abandoned them, and tells Lady Thornton that she is not fit to take care of evacuee children. Susan explains to Ada that it isn't right for Ada to take care of Susan on days like this, and that it is Susan who should be caring for Ada (p. 63).

As the book moves on, the two children and their caregiver slowly become more and more of a family, but that progression is punctuated by many moments in which their progress is erased as all three of them struggle to allow themselves to be cared for.

In chapter 16, Lady Thornton comes to Susan's house to thank Ada for her part in helping Lady Thornton's daughter Margaret, who had fallen from her horse and gotten a concussion. Although Lady Thornton is neither effusive nor nurturing, the scene is likely the first time in Ada's life when someone was thankful to her. Susan explains why Lady Thonton has come for a visit. Ada asks how Maggie is doing. Lady Thornton reports that Maggie is much better and thanks Ada, an action that seems to the reader to see a contrast to the efficient and perhaps aloof way that Lady Thornton usually comes across.

Besides saying thank you, Lady Thornton compliments Ada's horse-riding abilities, delivers a box of hand-me-down clothing for Ada and her brother, and invites Ada to discuss any questions she has about horses—with Lady Thornton's groom.

This is an awkward kind of thankfulness, but it is thankfulness nonetheless. Ada seems to view it as an odd moment and puts it out of her mind fairly quickly, but perhaps a seed gets planted. After all, if Lady Thornton can be grateful . . .

AS RELATIONSHIPS DEEPEN, THINGS DO NOT GET EASIER

After the first hundred pages or so of the book, the children's lives change dramatically. Jamie is going to school, and Ada, who was denied school by her Mam and is illiterate, divides her time between helping Susan around the house and riding Butter, Susan's pony. Riding horseback helps her feel what it is like to walk without pain. But the trauma from Ada and Jamie's earlier lives continues to haunt them and Susan still struggles with her grief for Becky. Ada's single biggest obstacle is her self-image. Susan asks Ada what sort of dress she would like Susan to make her for winter, suggesting blue or a specific shade of green that might complement Ada's complexion. Then Susan suggest velvet, remembering a dress she had made of that material when she was a girl and how much she loved that dress (p. 120).

Ada's response is a short statement that she hates velvet.

Susan laughs, knowing that Ada has no idea what velvet is. Susan asks Ada why she would say that. Ada replies that she doesn't want Susan to make things for her. When Susan asks why not, Ada doesn't reply, but thinks to herself that she is a feeble-minded girl, simple, not worth such clothing. She has also learned from growing up with Mam, that anything nice that is given can also be taken away as a punishment.

To Bradley's credit, she doesn't write the book in a way that allows for an easy fix. Ada's belief that she is worthless runs very deep, and her burgeoning fierceness can be read as coming from the conflict between how she sees herself, how Susan sees her, and how Ada will not let herself trust in anyone else. This conflict pops up in surprising ways.

One night at dinner, Susan notices welts on Jamie's hand. She suspects he is being bullied (which would account for his hatred of school and increased bed-wetting). The next day, Susan and Ada walk Jamie to school, then have tea in a small restaurant in the town (where Ada says thank you to her server, the first time in the book those words have crossed her lips.)

After their tea, Susan leads them back to the school and, with Ada in tow, walks into the schoolhouse and barges into Jamie's classroom. Susan is shocked to see that the teacher has tied Jamie's left hand to his desk to keep him from writing with that hand. Susan demands to know why the teacher would do such a thing. The teacher explains that left-handedness is of the devil and she must break him of it. Susan unties the hand and declares that such ideas are nonsense (citing one of her theology professors from her time at Oxford) and declares that if this ever happens again, she will take action.

But the more interesting moment occurs as Susan and Ada are walking home. Ada asks if her club foot might be of the devil too. Susan tries to explain to Ada how ridiculous that is, but at the same time realizes what she is up against, how deeply Ada has internalized her self-loathing.

Susan meanwhile, is struggling to push aside her own grief. When they have to register for identification cards as part of the war effort, Susan finds out that Ada and Jamie don't know their own birth dates. She picks birth dates for both of them and later admits to Ada that her birth date is Becky's birthday. Susan remarks that it would be a good thing to have a reason to celebrate that date again.

Ada accuses Susan of lying, because it won't really be nice to celebrate that day. Susan forces a laugh and explains that it is a lie and it also isn't. Susan knows that day will always be difficult for her, but she really wants it to be a happy day again. This admission, that Susan realizes she would like to move from grief into happiness (even though she may not be able to do so yet), represents a movement toward a position of thankfulness.

MOVING FORWARD AND BACKWARD AT THE SAME TIME

As was mentioned before, characters in this book tend to progress and digress at the same time. Ada becomes more aware of things that matter to her, things that she values. At the same time, she fears that if she appreciates things, she is vulnerable to losing them. Susan, who has lost the person she loved more than any other in the world, seems to have vowed to not put herself in the position of loss again, but while she was isolating herself from interaction with the community (and thus from romantic love), she hasn't realized that taking in two dirty, desperate children opens her up to another sort of vulnerability. Bradley captures the nonlinear ways that human growth works, including growth toward an awareness of thankfulness that reaches beyond self and others.

Susan seems to try to teach Ada to be thankful in herself and toward others. But we see in their interactions how every step forward involves at least one step back. When Ada is frustrated that no matter what she does, she is unable to get Butter, the pony, to move at anything faster than a walk, Susan suggests that Ada visit Grimes, Lady Thornton's groom, to ask advice.

Grimes sees the problem immediately. Susan has not been trimming Butter's hooves, which have grown so much that Butter is probably feeling pain with each step. As Grimes trims Butter's hooves, Ada searches her mind for the right words and finally speaks, giving a rather formal thank you to the groom. This expression of thanks is the first one she gives that seems not merely polite, but heartfelt, and she is thanking Grimes for helping Butter rather than for helping herself (though more cynical readers might point out that she will benefit from a horse that can walk without pain). Ada seems to have a real bond with Butter and is glad that Grimes can relieve this pain (p. 149).

If that is a movement toward a fuller type of thankfulness, however, Ada follows it up with a burning anger at Susan for neglecting the pony to the point where it cannot walk without hurting. It will not be hard for student readers to see that Ada's anger toward Susan is connected to her anger at Mam (who Ada now knows could have seen a doctor when Ada was a baby and surgically corrected Ada's club foot). She is mad at Susan for neglecting the pony and leaving it in a state like her own.

Similarly, caring for the children encourages Susan to take steps to rejoin the community she has abandoned. At the same time, doing so opens old wounds. For example, on page 159, when Ada asks Susan about her father, who Susan mentioned was a vicar in a church, Susan explains that her father has been clear that he believes that Susan's love for Becky means she is no longer redeemable. When Jamie asks what the word *redeemed* means. Susan replies that the word means she needs to change her sinful ways and get her heavenly crown back. It also means, she explains, that her parents don't like her. Jamie responds by saying that their Mam hates Ada and doesn't think she can be redeemed.

Although Ada and Jamie most likely have no idea that Susan is referring to her father's condemnation of her for loving another woman, it is clear that Susan's rejection by her parents hurts her deeply, in a way parallel to how Jamie and Ada's Mam's neglect and abuse has left them confused and broken. Student readers might also suggest a similarity between both Ada's and Susan's inability to change the quality of themselves that is causing their condemnation. Ada cannot prevent her having been born with a foot that doesn't work. Susan cannot change whom she loves.

Ada is becoming more aware of the things she deeply values. Her vulnerability seems sharper than Susan's (perhaps because Susan has lived with her pain for longer). When Ada thinks she has broken Susan's sewing machine. She hides under the bed in the spare room, terrified that Susan will hit her, or worse, that she will be sent back to Mam, without Jamie. As Ada hides under the bed, she becomes more and more panicky. She fears she will lose her horse, her newfound freedom, and her brother (p. 171). When Susan comes home, she eventually finds Ada and when Ada confesses, Susan assures her that she will be okay, regardless of what happens (p. 172). Ada doesn't believe her and is sure it everything isn't going to be okay.

Ada has come to care very deeply for the pony she may ride (who allows her to feel what it is like to walk without pain); for the freedom she has living with Susan where she is allowed to go outside and isn't locked in a cupboard (though, by hiding under the bed, she is imprisoning herself, albeit without roaches); and for being able to protect and care for her brother (though Susan has reassured her repeatedly that she doesn't have to care for Jamie, that is Susan's job now—though Susan doesn't understand that, for Ada, caring for Jamie is a part of her sense of self-worth). And while each of these elements she values have strings attached to them, acknowledging them is a big step toward thankfulness.

It is interesting that most of these things that she appreciates meet her basic needs—freedom from pain, a warm place to stay, food—but they represent a shift in her character. Even though (and maybe because) she fears losing them, these are things she values.

THANKFULNESS BECOMES MORE REAL

Until chapter 28 in the book, Ada's rare occasions of being thankful seem experimental and not entirely genuine. Susan and some other characters seem willing to give Ada and Jamie time to recover from the damage that Mam had done to them. At this point (roughly two-thirds of the way through the narrative) other characters begin to nudge them a bit more, and Ada seems to begin to want to show her thanks.

When Susan knits Ada some riding gloves with leather on the palms so she can hold the reins, Susan explains that she came up with the idea of how to make them and asks if Ada likes them. Ada's thoughts in the narration show hesitation, resistance, but also a giving in and a recognition that there are good gifts in life. Ada knows what she is supposed to say, but doesn't want to say it. She finally grudgingly admits that the gloves are okay. Then finally she thanks Susan.

Susan laughs, calls Ada a sourpuss, and ask if it would kill Ada to be thankful for once. In the narration, the reader hears (though Susan does not) Ada wondering if maybe it would kill her. She doesn't know (p. 190),

Even as Ada is taking the risk of being thankful, in spite of how that makes her vulnerable to losing it, so Susan, whose grief is sometimes thawing, sometimes still debilitating, also begins to risk thankfulness. Both Susan and Ada are learning thankfulness partly by caring for each other.

Susan tells Ada and Jamie that she usually feels unhappy and blue in the winter, as she was feeling when Jamie and Ada first came to her. But this winter she is too busy with shopping, cleaning, washing, sewing, and meetings to feel bad. Ada notices, however, that as winter becomes darker, Susan does seem blue. She was trying to be cheerful for Jamie and Ada, but Ada can tell that it is hard for her. Ada notices that Susan is always exhausted and tries to be helpful to her. Ada prepares meals and helps with the sewing and goes shopping with Susan.

Then on one particularly cold day, Ada notices Susan slumping in a chair. Ada sees that the fire is getting low, so she shovels in some coal and the fire comes to life again. Susan mutters her thanks (p. 195).

It would be interesting to ask student readers who this passage is primarily about. Susan, to be sure, is no longer alone, is allowing herself to be cared for, and is thankful for that. But perhaps more importantly, Ada is able to see outside of herself, outside of her own anxieties that she will return to a state of deprivation and abuse and see a chance to help someone who has helped her. Although Susan is the one who says thank you, in this scene, it may be Ada who is demonstrating the most thanks.

The closer Ada gets to a state of thankfulness, the more frightened she becomes. As winter sets in, Susan discovers that the children do not know much about Christmas. Ada describes it as a time when Mam would work late at the pub and they would eat better food for a couple of days. Susan takes the kids to cut down a Christmas tree, and then when they bring it home, she takes down a box of ornaments. As she opens them, though, Susan gets teary. These are ornaments she used to hang with Becky. Susan asks Ada if it would be okay if they would make their own ornaments.

Ada agrees, but the first-person narrative reveals what she is thinking. Christmas is making her anxious in ways she does not understand. Togetherness and celebrations feel threatening. She feels as though Christmas is something she should not be included in. Somehow, the fact that Susan wants her to be happy makes her even more anxious (p. 208).

THANKFULNESS AND RESPONSE

When *The War That Saved My Life* begins, Ada is motivated almost exclusively by the desire to survive and to protect her brother Jamie. Over the course of the book, as Susan shelters Ada, feeds her, keeps her safe, and shows her love, Ada continues to be able to see beyond herself. Through the book so far, we have seen a progression. First, Ada learns to say thank you out of politeness, but without necessarily meaning it. Next, Ada begins to genuinely appreciate the other people in her life, and learns how to say thank you with genuine heartfelt words and with actions that show her appreciation.

The final turn, as we near the end of the book, is that Ada begins to act generously, out of thankfulness, toward those she does not know and those who have not necessarily done anything for her.

We'll begin considering the change in the way Ada acts toward those she knows. In discussion with Maggie, Ada decides she would like to make Susan a Christmas present. She asks Fred, the groom, if he has any wool she could have. He gives her his wife's knitting bag and explains that his wife died several years ago and would be pleased if someone could use it. Ada turns to go, then Fred, with a gentle smile, stops her and explains that when you receive a gift, you are supposed to say thank you (p. 210).

Ada realizes that Susan had taught her to do that, but she had been so busy thinking about the wool in the bag that she had forgotten. But what she says shows more than a minimum of polite words. She thanks Fred twice and tells him she wishes she could tell his late wife her thanks as well (p. 211). And it isn't just that Ada has learned to say the words of thanks. She is also demonstrating thankfulness in her actions. Ada works on Susan's present in secret, practicing first on a hat for Jamie.

On Christmas Eve, Susan gives Ada a handmade velvet dress. Ada puts it on and thinks it is beautiful. But when Susan says the dress is perfect and tells Ada that she looks beautiful it leads Ada down a dark and traumatic train of thought. She begins hearing her Mam in her head calling her ugly and filthy and nothing more than trash, reminding her that no one will ever care for her because of her horrible foot (p. 213). Ada begins to panic, not knowing why. She starts screaming and kicking and clawing and can't stop. Susan holds her, perhaps for hours, Ada can't be sure, until finally Ada calms down.

The next morning, Ada finds herself with a blanket wrapped tight around her, sleeping in the living room, and sees Susan sleeping in an armchair, with scratches and welts on her face and her clothing torn. She worries of Susan's anger, but when Susan wakes up, she reassures Ada that she isn't mad and tells Ada it wasn't her fault that she was scared. Shortly after that, Ada gives Susan the handmade scarf that she knitted in secret. Susan unfolds it and looks at it, then remarks that the scarf is beautiful and asks if this is what Ada has been up to (p. 220).

Ada tells Susan she got the wool from Fred so Susan will know she didn't steal it. Susan hugs her and says she loves it and will wear it every day. The scarf is a physical manifestation of two things, Ada's thankfulness (or maybe even love) and the time and effort she took to make it. This certainly seems like a shift in who Ada is and how she interacts with the world.

Even though she feels uncomfortable in the beautiful velvet dress, she wears it later in the day when they host three British pilots from the airfield across the field for Christmas dinner. Ada wears the dress because she knows it will make Susan happy (though Susan at one point quietly acknowledges that she can tell it is hard for Ada.) When one of the pilot's compliments her dress, Ada says thank you.

After Christmas, she finally accepts the invitation to tea from the old blind colonel and her friend and fellow evacuee, Stephen (it is the third time she has been invited) and expresses her thankfulness for the invitation and the scones they eat (Stephen and the colonel had saved their butter ration to make the scones) (p. 238).

And when they celebrate Ada's birthday and Susan gives Ada a secondhand book inscribed to her with love, and Ada's friend Maggie gives her a carved wooden pony, in that moment, Ada thinks in the narration that she has been given so much, and that makes her feel so sad. Somehow, the way Mam has raised her continues to twist the way Ada feels and sees herself and the world.

When the Dunkirk evacuation happens and their coastal village is overrun by wounded and dying soldiers, Ada works all day and well into the night carrying water and tea to the wounded. It is hard work and involves seeing blood, smelling urine and waste, and sometimes seeing soldiers die. Ada does that work though, not to impress Susan or anybody else, but because she desperately wants to help the soldiers. She has turned her focus outward, and her awareness of thankfulness seems to be prompting her to do good and thoughtful things.

THE ENDING AND LECTIO DIVINA

The War That Saved My Life, of course, doesn't end with a moment of thankful acknowledgment of all that Susan has done for Ada and Jamie (or of all Ada and Jamie have done for Susan, or of all the community has done for all of them). The closest moment to that happens about 50 pages from the end of the book.

How might we have a look at how we might use Lectio Divina to help students analyze this passage as part of a book that is a prayer of thankfulness? This passage occurs during a quiet moment in the middle of the night, when Ada wakes up, comes downstairs, and finds that Susan is awake. Shortly thereafter, Susan confesses that she had worried for a long time that she was neglecting Ada and Jamie. She wasn't taking care of them they way she remember her mother taking care of her—constantly watching her, and making sure that her appearance was always perfect. Susan reflects that her mother would never have let a child run wild the way Susan has let Ada run wild.

But upon reflection, Susan decides that maybe she didn't do that bad of a job after all. She doubts that Ada would have liked being taken care of the way Susan's mother took care of her.

Ada says she is unsure of how to respond. When she isn't thinking about how she has been raised by Susan, everything seems clear. But as soon as she reflects upon it, everything becomes confused.

Susan says she feels that way too. But then something happens that hasn't happened yet in the book. Ada leans against Susan and Susan puts an arm around her, and as Ada becomes drowsy and finally slips into slumber, she feels Susan kiss the top of her head (p. 264–65).

To lead a Lectio Divina exercise on this passage, the teacher might break students up into partner groups or small groups and have them discuss and report. In this case, we will describe a whole-class exercise. For each question, the teacher asks students to write a brief informal response, then call on those writings in the discussion. The teacher then asks the first question:

What is going on in this passage? What is the literal meaning of this passage?

Students will have a variety of ways of describing the scene and contributing details from the text. One student, Kathryn, reads from what she wrote, describing the scene as a pretty straightforward moment. Susan is reflecting on her own upbringing, confiding in Ada how she felt at first that she was neglecting Ada and Jamie, then describing how she realized that she had perhaps done a better job than she thought.

Another student, Frances, isn't so sure the moment is straightforward. She notices that when Susan asks Ada what she thinks, the scene doesn't go as we might expect it to. This is the moment in the story when we might expect Ada to thank Susan and reassure her that she has done a fine job of being a caregiver—except that would not be in keeping with who Ada is. Ada's answer, in the end, is that she doesn't know, that she is confused. But then Ada tentatively leans her head against Susan. As Susan does not push her away, Ada leans in even more. Susan puts her arm around Ada. Ada then nestles in and falls asleep.

Eli reads from his journal response that the scene is about both of them experiencing moments of vulnerability.

The teacher then suggests that they move on to the next category of questions and consider:

> What allegorical meaning can student readers find in this text? In other words, what stories, images, songs, archetypes, myths, or memes does this passage remind them of?

It is important to remember that for these exercises or methods to work, the teacher has to be open to whatever insights the students might bring. So while lesson plans might describe what teachers expect students to bring forward, based on the teacher's own interpretation, the teacher should remain flexible and value what insights emerge from the discussion.

The teacher calls on Landon, who connects Ada's actions with a genuine thankfulness and comfort that she cannot articulate.

Favour sees the real answer to Susan's question in the way they nestle together. And they might see that both Ada and Susan are yearning for something.

After reading some student responses, and discussing other insights students have noticed, the teacher proceeds to the third question:

> How can student readers connect this passage to their own lives? What implications are there in this passage for how student readers understand, remember, or value their experiences in the world?

The teacher gives students a little longer than the usual ten minutes for writing because many students are still writing at the usual cut-off time. Eventually, the teacher brings the writing to a close and opens up the floor for discussion. Ryan talks about how he was bullied in middle school and how hard it was for him to trust relationships after that. He sees a parallel to Ada's unwillingness to trust that things will get better.

Jae raises her had. Jae is usually shy but asks if they can read their journal entry. They read about what life was like before their father left, how he seemed nice sometimes, but other times was violent. They understand how Ada might have a hard time being thankful for anything after that. Other students talk about betrayal by friends and anger and grief at losing someone they loved. The teacher notices the time and cuts the discussion short to get in the final question before the bell.

The teacher asks students to respond in writing once more, this time to the final question of lectio divina,

> What is this text inviting student readers to do?

To be fair, the primary purpose of a novel is not to inspire action, though one might argue that young adult novels, perhaps because of the audience, tend to bring about reflection that often does result in action.

Once again, the teacher asks students to write a response. This time the teacher only gives them five minutes, reasoning that this question does not lead to narrative answers as often. When the time is over, the teacher asks for responses. Predictably, some students respond that the story calls on them to be more thankful in their own lives. Others, however write about how they see a lot of selfishness in the world, and how maybe the book is saying we need to think about thankfulness in a different, bigger way. Verity says she needs to use thankfulness to think about how we can live our lives for others more.

The teacher doesn't have time to hear from all the students, and has to make do with those who have been called on. We cannot imagine the whole range of responses that this question might elicit in your students, but students may reflect on relationships in their own lives, might think about how they think about people like Ada, or consider how they might be able to help people the way Susan does, or think about what sort of family they wish to gather about themselves. In his own teaching, Bill has found, in using this approach in class, that a passage like the one above is likely to draw out responses that are both engaging and touching—and often such connections, if students have the time to write them up, are remarkably moving.

ENDINGS

The War That Saved My Life offers a great deal to talk about when viewed as a prayer of thanks. Viewing Ada and Susan's separate journeys to a position of thankfulness might be thought of as a *wicked problem*. Horst Rittel and Melvin Webber, two design theorists, are credited with introducing the term in 1973. Simply put, a wicked problem, unlike a chess or mathematical problem, is hard to formulate, doesn't have an internal logic that signals when it is done, does not have a testable solution, cannot be solved through trial and error, has more than one solution, is sometimes symptomatic of other problems, and solutions to it cannot be declared to be right or wrong (Rittel & Webber, 1973).

Good teachers look for problems like these. They allow students to think hard about subjects that are complicated and can bear thinking and rethinking about. Looking at how Ada and Susan change (and don't change) over the course of the book is a wicked problem. Students can see the ways in which their own journey is equally complicated. And other books can also be viewed with this approach. As we have said elsewhere in this book, considering a YA book as a prayer (in this case a prayer of thanks) will open your students to richer, broader discussions which, while perhaps being less predictable, will not only make your class more exciting to your students, but will strengthen their critical and writing abilities as well.

Chapter 7

Louisiana's Way Home and *The Poet X* as Prayers of Reconciliation

The concept of reconciliation comes from the Greek word *katallage,* which means "an exchange; restoration to favor; change" (Sauter, 2005, p. 504). Sauter observes that throughout Christian theology, reconciliation describes the restored relationship between humans and God or between humans themselves. In the Catholic tradition, the sacrament of reconciliation consists of conversion, confession, and celebration and is often referred to as a sacrament of healing. Other traditions, including Judaism and Islam, include reconciliation as an important component of their religious observance.

Reconciliation often includes disappointments, setbacks, and the need to persist over a long time. It also includes other emotions such as anger, lament, grief, and confession. It's not an automatic process and depends on the attitudes and actions of those involved. Accepting responsibility for one's actions, desiring to make things right, showing evidence of a change in behavior, being willing to make restitution where needed, and rebuilding trust are all needed in order for reconciliation to occur. Ultimately it requires hope and trust.

While reconciliation and forgiveness are often lumped together, in fact forgiveness is usually regarded as a part of reconciliation. Both are responses to a broken relationship, reconciliation extends beyond forgiveness to also include repairing and restoring what once was, or proceeding from brokenness to something different and better.

Upon first glance, the middle grade novel *Louisiana's Way Home* by two-time Newbery Medalist Kate DiCamillo, and the National Book Award and Carnegie Medal–winning young adult novel, *The Poet X* by Elizabeth Acevedo, do not have a lot in common. *Louisiana's Way Home* is about Louisiana, a 12-year-old white girl, who unexpectedly leaves her home in

Florida with her grandmother and ends up in Georgia. *The Poet X* is a coming of age story about Xiomara, a 16-year-old Dominican American girl from Harlem who learns to find her own voice as she navigates her way through the complicated relationships around her.

The settings, characters, and contexts in these two books are very different from each other, but we suggest that both of these stories can be read as prayers of reconciliation, in which characters learn to forgive those who have hurt them and start the process of repairing and restoring broken relationships. Louisiana and Xiomara each embark on a journey of reconciliation with the mother figures in their lives—Louisiana and her grandmother, Xiomara and her mom. Both told in first person, the stories trace the ways that the reconciliation process is long and difficult for Louisiana and Xiomara.

While we are not privy to the inner thoughts and feelings of Louisiana's grandmother and Xiomara's mother, readers can infer their participation in the process, a process that changes all of them and the ways they see themselves and others.

Some storylines wrap up conflicts between characters in simplified and contrived ways. These stories do not. Rather, they reveal the truth and complexity of reconciliation, a process that is profound and beautiful but not simple, easy, or final.

LOUISIANA'S WAY HOME

Louisiana's Way Home is the story of Louisiana Elefante, a 12-year-old orphan who lives with her grandmother. Set in Florida in 1977, Louisiana describes her story as being one of sorrow and confusion and yet at the same time a story of happiness, kind actions, and gifted peanuts (p. 17–18). Readers first encountered Louisiana in DiCamillo's *Raymie Nightingale* (2016), as one of Raymie's best friends. This story, however, is Louisiana's alone.

The book begins with Louisiana's grandmother waking her up in the middle of the night and telling her that it is time for confronting and reckoning with the curse and that they need to leave immediately. They get in the car and set out on a road trip. Louisiana doesn't know where they are going or for how long, but is used to the ideas her grandmother has in the middle of the night and goes along with it.

After falling asleep in the car, Louisiana wakes up and realizes that they are now in Georgia and far from home. She starts worrying about all they've left behind, including her beloved cat Archie, but her grandmother assures her that she has made arrangements for all of that and that Louisiana doesn't have to worry. Louisiana doesn't believe her grandmother and starts to cry.

When she tries to convince her grandmother to turn around and drive back home, her grandmother refuses. This is no surprise to Louisiana because, as she reflects, her Granny is the sort of person who gives instructions rather than taking them. The whole situation causes Louisiana to feel both desperate and devastated and deeply angry at her grandmother. She just wants to go home to her friends.

The road trip takes an abrupt stop when Granny experiences severe tooth pain and needs emergency dental surgery. They find a dentist in Richford, Georgia who pulls out all of Granny's teeth, resulting in Granny and Louisiana being stuck in a hotel room while Granny recuperates. During this time, Louisiana earns money for the hotel stay by singing at funerals at a local church and encounters many interesting people along the way.

Acknowledging the Brokenness

On one level, Louisiana and her grandmother need reconciliation because of her grandmother's decision to take her on the road trip. Louisiana is very angry at her grandmother for taking her away from her home, her pets, and her friends Raymie and Beverly. She refuses to look at her grandmother during their road trip and repeatedly tells her that she doesn't believe in her grandmother's attempts to reassure her. She vows to never speak to her, to ask her a question, or ever to forgive her (pp. 34, 53). She surmises that her grandmother doesn't care about what she wants.

It soon becomes clear, however, that Louisiana's anger toward her grandmother has been simmering for a long time. Living with Granny over the years has not been easy for Louisiana, and she harbors hard feelings toward her. The ways that Granny brought her up were unconventional to say the least and, increasingly, it had bothered Louisiana. She is bothered by how much her grandmother manipulates and takes advantage of people, borrows things without returning them, and sometimes outright steals things (p. 12). Louisiana is tired of putting up with this and is ready to speak out (p. 94).

In addition, Granny repeatedly talks about a curse that her great-grandfather put into motion generations ago, a curse that Granny thinks dictates all that happens to them and believes is their legacy. Louisiana doubts its validity.

As the story progresses, we learn that there is even more for Louisiana to get angry about. When she comes back to the hotel one afternoon, she finds out that Granny has abandoned her. All that is left is a letter from Granny in which she explains how everything Louisiana knows about her past is a lie. Granny writes that she has gone to find Elf Ear, the birthplace of her grandfather, to confront the curse and needs to do this alone. She also tells Louisiana that she is not her blood relative. She found Louisiana as an abandoned baby in an alley behind a five-and-dime store on a pile of cardboard boxes. Louisiana is dumbfounded, confused, and angry.

Support from Friends

As the story progresses, Louisiana encounters a myriad of people who help her process her complicated and raw feelings and show her love and kindness. She meets a mysterious boy with a crow on his shoulders, Burke Allen, who becomes her friend and allows her to be hopeful (p. 69). Burke introduces her to his family and they welcome her in as one of their own. His mom, Carole Ann, helps Louisiana see that there are people in the world who have goodness in their hearts (p. 56).

Louisiana also meets Bernice, the hotel owner, Ms. Lulu the church organist, and the Reverend Frank Obertask, all of whom treat Louisiana differently than her grandmother does. Meeting these people and benefiting from their abundant generosity and kindness helps Louisiana clarify the brokenness in her relationship with her grandmother, the lack of trust and love they seem to have with each other.

At one point, Reverend Obertask encourages her to talk through what is going on. He suggests it might help her to feel better and begin healing if she tells him (p. 164). Later, he encourages her to forgive her grandmother and her parents. He tells her that she will never fully understand why her parents abandoned her in an alley. But he suggests that she may be able to forgive them, and that doing so will help her (p. 199).

But Louisiana is not ready, at this point, to forgive. She is still angry toward her grandmother, her parents, and to the curse for determining this series of unfortunate events in her life. She wonders how she could ever forgive people who have never been kind or loving to her (p. 199).

Incremental Progress

It is only when Louisiana starts changing the way she sees herself and her situation that she is able to forgive and work toward reconciliation. She realizes she is clever and able and that the curse doesn't need to determine the events of her life.

We see glimpses of this change when Louisiana agrees to sing at the funeral of a stranger. While singing, she imagines seeing her Granny in the audience and hears Granny affirming her in her talent for singing.

Another important step is that Louisiana acknowledges that Granny has told her she was a good singer. Granny often tells her that she has a gift and that the more she can put herself into her singing, the stronger and more real the song becomes (p. 185). Granny was able to see something in Louisiana that Louisiana wasn't able to see in herself. Louisiana reflects on this and recognizes that the realization that she could sing was something that her Granny had given her (p. 214).

At the end of the story, we realize that Louisiana has been writing down the events of the novel as a letter to her grandmother. She tells Granny that she has decided to stay with the Allens and that the Reverend puts her in touch with her friends in Florida, who come to visit her. Once bitterly angry at her grandmother, Louisiana has come to acknowledge the love that Granny has shown her.

She is able to better understand Granny's explanation in the letter that Granny had named her for where she was found and that taking care of her was the high point of Granny's life. Granny also explained that she really and truly loved Louisiana (p. 122–23). Louisiana now understands that Granny gave her many things and, in her own crazy way, was trying to keep Louisiana safe and healthy.

Louisiana ends the story by saying that she loves Granny and forgives her (p. 227). Louisiana has been able to forgive her grandmother and also recognize the love her grandmother has shown her. While there isn't a neat and tidy ending, Louisiana and her grandmother have been able to reconcile with each other. Louisiana's story is a story of a reconciliation journey, a journey that involves brokenness and pain but also forgiveness and love.

THE POET X

The Poet X is a story in verse of first generation Dominican American Xiomara Batista, who lives in Harlem. It is broken up into three parts. In part 1 of the book ("In the Beginning Was the Word"), we meet the main characters and are introduced to the main conflicts. Part 2, "And the Word Was Made Flesh," delves into the conflicts particularly between Xiomara and her mom, and part 3, "The Voice of One Crying in the Wilderness," shows resolutions to these conflicts. As such, this book can be read as a prayer of reconciliation and a journey from brokenness to wholeness.

When the story begins, we learn that Xiomara is used to standing out because her body is no longer that of a young girl (p. 5). She doesn't feel known or seen beyond the limiting ways boys and grown men look at her and harass her. In response to this, she has learned to be tough and unbreakable. Always ready to fend off and respond to unwelcome advances, she hides her insecurities and questions.

Xiomara lives with her mother, Altagracia Batista, her father, and her twin brother, Twin. While her brother plays the role of the good child, Xiomara frequently lives out the meaning of her name, which means ready for battle, with her resistance to her mother's strict rules. Her mother expects Xiomara to do the housekeeping after school (unlike her twin brother), doesn't allow her to date, frequently criticizes her, and closely monitors her comings and goings. In addition, her mother, a devout Catholic, expects her children to obey the rules and practices of the church and leaves no room for Xiomara to question or doubt.

Xiomara has many questions and doubts about who she is, who she wants to be, and where God fits into all of this. When Mami starts pressuring her to complete her confirmation as a Catholic, Xiomara doesn't feel ready for this and isn't even sure if this is something she wants to do. She feels shame about her body because of language in church and gets herself into trouble in communion class by explaining why she does not believe the Bible is literal or true.

She reflects, "Just seems as I got older, I began to really see the way that church treats a girl like me differently" (p. 14). She struggles with the different messages that women and girls seem to be told compared to that of men and boys, and this makes her "feel so small" (p. 58). She asks, "What's the point of God giving me life if I can't live it as my own?" (p. 57). The trouble is that Xiomara isn't sure how to share these questions and struggles with Mami.

Starting to Do the Work

Xiomara's journey toward reconciliation with her mother parallels her journey of finding her own voice, of being able to articulate the pain she has experienced and advocate for herself. In this, Ms. Galiano, Xiomara's English teacher, plays a big role. Ms. Galiano encourages Xiomara to write down her feelings and explore the world of spoken word poetry. Xiomara has always written in a journal. However, it takes a long time before she is able to see herself as a poet and feel confident enough to share her writing with others. She reflects that often it seems that writing is the only thing that keeps her from hurting (p. 41).

Spoken word poetry provides Xiomara with a space for her to express her innermost questions, passions, frustrations, and doubts without worry of punishment or shame from her mother or others. After watching a spoken word poet perform, Xiomara writes in her journal, "We're different, this poet and I. In looks, in body, in background. But I don't feel so different when I listen to her. I feel heard" (p. 76). When she starts attending the poetry club, Xiomara begins to form a community with its other members and grows increasingly confident about sharing her work.

In her writing, Xiomara shares insights into her mother's background that give us a better understanding of some of her mother's fears and concerns.

For years, her mother and father were unable to have children. When the twins were born, they rejoiced about the miracle that had happened. Their prayers had been answered. This was a clear indication that God loved them (p. 18). In an effort to provide for her two miracles from God, Mami works long hours as a cleaning lady, unnoticed by those around her, and comes home exhausted.

Xiomara, however, is not able to empathize with her mother yet. For now, her mother's actions toward her are only unfair and unkind. And, while Father Sean gives her space to admit her doubts with the church and its teachings and express her strong emotions, Xiomara isn't able to do this yet either. He tells Xiomara that everyone doubts themselves at some point. He encourages her to find comfort in the forgiveness that religion can provide. He tells her that the church cares about her and is ready to support her (p. 123). But Xiomara isn't ready yet to hear this. She is not ready to forgive her mother or see religion as welcoming space within which to forgive.

A Slow Process

Conflicts between Xiomara and Mami increase dramatically when Mami sees Xiomara and her new secret boyfriend, Aman, kissing on a train. Mami makes Xiomara kneel on uncooked grains of rice in front of her altar to the Virgin Mary until Xiomara's knees are bloody as punishment. She restricts what Xiomara can do and only allows her to go to school and church. This makes Xiomara so angry that she no longer wants to be around her mom.

Xiomara continues to write poetry as a way to sort out her feelings and, as part of this, is able to remember many of the good times she has had with Mami. She remembers the fun they had ice skating together (p. 184) and remembers when her mother was her hero (p. 179). In the privacy of her journal and own thoughts, she acknowledges Mami's strength and resilience. She recalls her mom praising how she works hard and is so patient (p. 211) and is proud of this. Though she writes about their relationship, Xiomara is unable to speak her feelings of love and gratitude to her mom. Instead, she focuses on how their relationship has changed since Xiomara became a teenager.

During this time, Father Sean provides a listening ear and acts as a liaison between her and Mami. He convinces Mami that Xiomara is not ready for confirmation class, thus freeing her up to attend the poetry class. He encourages Xiomara to forgive her mother, saying "Our God is a forgiving God. Even when we do things we shouldn't, our God understands the weakness of the flesh. But forgiveness is only granted if the person is actually remorseful. I think this goes much deeper than kissing a boy on the train" (p. 227). In saying this, he nudges Xiomara to consider that there is more at play here than getting in trouble for kissing a boy.

Xiomara begins to show signs of remorse and wrestles with what she should do. She reflects that she never meant to hurt anyone and defines herself as someone who is acting or pretending all the time. She pretends she is unable to see what is around her. She pretends that everything is okay, when it isn't. She wonders if she is worthy of forgiveness (p. 235). Mami also starts showing a willingness to reconcile. She gives Xiomara a present, a baby bracelet resized into a necklace (p. 291) as a tangible expression of her love for her daughter.

This book is not only about Xiomara's journey through the process of reconciliation, but also is about her journey to understand that process. Her poetry allows her to describe what she is feeling, but also lets her reflect on what she should do.

No Tidy Ending

Reconciliation in *The Poet X* does not magically occur in the end, nor does it solve all the conflicts between Xiomara and Mami. Rather, the book acknowledges that Xiomara's journey toward forgiveness does not resolve everything. In fact, at the very end of the story is when things become their worst. At school one day, Xiomara realizes that she left her journal on the kitchen table (p. 298). She comes home to find that Mami has read it. In front of Xiomara, Mami burns the journal, disgusted by what she has read in it.

Mami asks Xiomara if she really thought that Mami couldn't read enough English to know that Xiomara was talking about boys and church and Mami herself in the diary (p. 300). Though Xiomara tries to explain that the journal is just her personal thoughts and that the words are private (p. 302) and that she is sorry about what she wrote, Mami refuses to listen.

This causes Xiomara to finally share all her feelings out loud with her mom. As her mom quotes the Bible to Xiomara, she gets angry and starts yelling back. Xiomara compares the conflict with a battlefield as the two women throw grenades of violent words at each other (p. 308).

Xiomara leaves home and stays the night at Aman's house. When she returns to school, Ms Galiano encourages her to figure out how to talk to her mom so they can figure out how to heal their relationship (p. 333). Xiomara makes the decision to do this and goes back home, inviting Aman, Caridad, Savier, and Father Sean with her. When she sees her mom, she tells her that they have to discuss things, and that she thinks they need help to do that (p. 338). Though Xiomara has lots of questions about her faith, she includes Father Sean into the conversation.

When Mami sees her, they embrace in a hug, Xiomara realizing that their arms can reach each other and comfort with hugs in ways that words are incapable of doing: "Can hug tight" (p. 340). Her mom isn't ready yet to say sorry or that she loves Xiomara but when she pat's Xiomara's back with strength and runs her hand through Xiomara's hair, Xiomara reflects that it is enough for now. While they have not fully reconciled, there is hope, and they are both committed fully to the process.

In the weeks that follow, Xiomara and Mami continue to work on their relationship and toward reconciliation. They meet with regularly with Father Sean to talk together. At times, the whole family participates in these meetings and it is good for all of their relationships. They learn more about each other and what it is like to see things from their perspectives.

The story ends with Xiomara performing one of her poems at the Citywide Slam Poetry Contest with her family and friends in the audience supporting her and cheering her one. They celebrate together and her mother proclaims that they are only going to move forward from this point, not backward (p. 355). While there isn't a tidy ending or an end point, there is a vision of a relationship that is healing and stronger than before.

USING MARGINALIA TO EXPLORE RECONCILIATION

Both *Louisiana's Way Home* and *The Poet X* explore the complexities involved in reconciliation. In our conversations with students about these books, we've found it helpful to use the sacred text reading practice of marginalia to help identify and discuss these complexities.

Marginalia is the practice of making marks or comments in the margins of books. While the first recorded use of marginalia occurs in *Blackwood's Magazine* in 1819 (Oxford English Dictionary, n.d.), it is a practice that occurred even before the invention of the printing press. When books were copied by hand, readers often wrote notes in the margins of the books to help later readers better understand what they read.

In 1996, American Poet Laureate Billy Collins wrote a poem about marginalia titled "Poem Hunter." So marginalia is not a new technique, nor one that is not already known. However, while its use is widespread in AP classes in the United States, usually marginalia is a solitary activity, allowing individual readers to reflect as they read a text. In their podcast, Zoltan and ter Kuile may have pioneered the use of it as a discussion technique (and certainly popularized it).

Marginalia encompasses comments, questions, criticism, annotations, or drawings in books. Annotations can be assessments of the work as a whole, ongoing reactions to what has been read, summaries of the contents of a chapter, or a reaction to a section of the book. Marginalia can also include a readers' index, a list of page numbers at the end of the book representing parts of the book that readers want to come back to or that represent key ideas.

A conventional practice is for readers to write down comments as they come upon them, the page references, and a word or two to indicate the subject of the passage noted. Readers can mark particular words or passages, jot down headings, create an index, underline a word, or mark a passage. They can argue with the text, address questions directly to the author or character, or make comments to oneself. Annotations can be made in the front or back pages of the book, or in the space at the start of a new chapter or section. Recording annotations on Post-It notes can be a way of annotating library books or class sets of books that need to be reused.

Reading someone else's annotations can serve different purposes. When reading someone else's annotations, a number of inferences can be made. The total number of notes may be an indication of the degree of the earlier reader's interest. The kinds of comments can suggest the kinds of things or themes the reader was looking for or reacted to. Reading others' annotations can connect readers across time and space and offer new ways to think about the shared text, and can offer different reactions to it.

While marginalia can be done with any book, *The Poet X* and *Louisiana's Way Home* are particularly suited for this practice because of how they are written. Both books have wide margins on their pages—*The Poet X* because it is written in poetry, and *Louisiana's Way Home* because of DiCamillo's sparse writing style and short chapters (which often straddles the distinction between poetry and prose). In addition, because the concept of reconciliation is complicated and at times messy, there is much to respond to and reflect on as readers both identify and react to the reconciliation journeys of our protagonists.

In addition to the specific way of using marginalia that is described, Deb has expanded on Daniels et al.'s (2007) concept of a "Write Around" as a way to use marginalia in the classroom. She has found success with it because it encourages each student to record their own annotations in response to a text and to respond to others' annotations.

To do this activity, divide students into groups of three to five and create a string of conversations around passages from the book that were chosen by students. Students can write in their own books, or photocopies of particular chapters or pages of the book can be distributed to students, but each student should have a copy of the text. It works best, in Deb's experience, to do this activity after students have read the entire book or by choosing a chapter or series of pages on which to focus the annotations. Teachers can focus on chapters that foreground factors contributing to both Louisiana's and Xiomara's decisions to reconcile.

Ask students to write their thoughts, questions, reactions, and/or feelings to the passage from the book for approximately one minute. Next, have them pass their books or papers to the person sitting beside them. They then read the new annotations and write a reaction, response, comment, objection, affirmation, or raise a new idea to keep the conversation going. Give approximately one minute for this as well. Continue doing this for four times until each person's initial comment sheet returns to them.

Once this happens, each student reads all the group members' comments stemming from their original annotations. Each group member summarizes the written conversation and then the conversation continues from that point aloud in the classroom.

Once the write around activity has gone through a round or two. The teacher might stop the activity and then ask students to find agreement or connections within a string of two to five related comments. When it is that group's turn, the group reads the comment string to the rest of the class. The teacher then asks students how this comment helps them to think new thoughts, reactions, or reflections about the theme of reconciliation.

While marginalia does not necessarily lend itself to quick-moving discussions where outgoing and excited students build upon each other's ideas quickly or have engaging disagreement, this approach encourages thoughtful reflection. Teachers should encourage students to be as comfortable as they can with silence as their classmates reflect.

Understanding reconciliation in both *Louisiana's Way Home* and *The Poet X* is a process that requires recursive reflection and encourages close reading by asking students to notice particular aspects of the text. Marginalia and the write around activity allows students to work together to address difficult topics, and encourages thoughtful consideration that will benefit your students as they come to understand YA texts more deeply.

Chapter 8

Using Havruta to Consider *Orbiting Jupiter* and *The Beast Player* as Prayers of Obedience

A prayer of obedience might seem like an odd thing. After all, there are plenty of examples in various holy scriptures of people praying prayers of thanks, prayers of confession, prayers asking for forgiveness, but are there ever any prayers for obedience? The answer is that there are, often on behalf of a community. It might be hard to imagine from the perspective of an individualistic, sometimes Darwinian, or even Machiavellian, Western society—but holy scriptures, particularly the books of the judges in Christian and Jewish traditions, are filled with pleas from leaders that God would help his people learn to obey.

Orbiting Jupiter, by Gary Schmidt, was long-listed for the Carnegie Medal in 2017. Schmidt is also a two-time Newbery Honor winner. The YA novel is told from the point of view of Jack, whose family agrees to take in a foster child named Joseph. Joseph has fathered a daughter with a girl his age. Since then he has entered the foster care system, assaulted a teacher, spent time in a juvenile detention center, missed the birth of his child, and now wants nothing more than to be reunited with Madeleine, the child's mother, and Jupiter, his daughter. He carries trauma with him from the juvenile center and has to learn how to live with a family and survive in a new school.

Schmidt has published many other middle grade and young adult novels including *Wednesday Wars* (2007), *Trouble* (2008), *Okay for Now* (2011), *Pay Attention Carter Jones* (2019), and *Just Like That* (2021).

Nahoko Uehashi's *The Beast Player*, translated from the Japanese by Cathy Hirano, won both the Prinz Honor and the Batchelder Award in 2020. The protagonist, Elin, whose mother cares for the powerful water serpents that defend the kingdom, is accused of killing some of the creatures and is sentenced to death. Elin's mother puts Elin on one of the beasts and sends her to another kingdom far away. Elin barely survives the journey, but a kind old schoolteacher finds and raises her. As she grows up, she finds she has an affinity for the winged creatures that protect her adopted kingdom. Elin discovers something about the beasts that may threaten their safety and hers as well.

Uehashi has also published a sequel to *The Beast Player* titled *The Beast Warrior* (2020).

Both Schmidt and Uehashi use scenes of disobedience as well as obedience. Characters of both books are torn between two different sets of laws, values, commands, requirements, or requests. Each book, however, approaches disobedience and obedience in different ways. *Orbiting Jupiter* focuses on individual obedience. In its pages, we see societal understandings of obedience as a chore, as a matter of power, as an annoyance, as an infringement upon freedom, and as a reflection of love. In *The Beast Player*, obedience is socially constructed as a calling, a lifelong burden, and a deep responsibility to community.

We have written already about different discussion methods for considering sacred text in the classroom. We have explained and given examples of how to use different sacred text methods to guide students' discussion of single chapters and in terms of the whole book. By focusing on small moments and passages, sometimes only a sentence or two, students can keep the focus on the text while discussing themes that echo through every other page of the book. In this chapter, we consider the potential for using havruta to introduce discussion and comparisons between the two books—seeing how the two different books feature different understandings of obedience. This practice can help students explore these books as prayers of obedience.

In chapter 6 we considered how havruta might help students consider the theme of equanimity in *brown girl dreaming*. Havruta is an ancient Jewish practice of repeated readings that slowly builds interpretive understanding. When havruta is engaged in a whole-class context, students begin by picking a passage. The teacher (or the class) narrows down the nominated passages to anywhere from one to four, depending on how much time is available.

Once the passages have been chosen, the teacher asks each student who identified a passage to give the rest of the class the context of the quote and tell the class what that passage reminded them of or how it connects to them. The teacher then opens the discussion up to the whole group to see what thoughts or ideas it causes them to think. The teacher might initially have students write out their responses, then share them with the larger group.

TEACHING *ORBITING JUPITER* WITH HAVRUTA

In the unit that Bill taught, he began with *Orbiting Jupiter*, but of course you could begin with either book (and for that matter, you might choose to use havruta for one of the books and a different sacred reading practice for the other book). After reading *Orbiting Jupiter*, Bill's students came up with four passages connected to the theme of obedience that they were interested in investigating. Those passages included:

1. A sentence from page 7 in which Jack's dad tells Joseph that there is something he needs to finish, in reference to milking the cow (p. 7).
2. A quote from Joseph's dad when he encounters Jack outside the farmhouse and observes that Jack must be being forced to do chores and asks what Jack did to get punished by being sent to the farmhouse (p. 30).
3. Another quote from Joseph's dad in which he claims that the family has taken Joseph in only for the income that foster parenting provides (p. 128).
4. And finally a quote from Jupiter's foster mother asking Jack to tell Joseph that Jupiter is doing well, that she is learning and developing, that she is happy, and that she needs a family. Jupiter's foster mother then asks Joseph and his father to give up their attempts to get custody of Jupiter (p. 154–55).

OBEDIENCE AND RESPECT

What follows is a recreation of an actual class discussion based on notes Bill took in class. Though the quotations from students are not word-for-word, they are true to the ideas that students brought up. For ease of reading, we have given the students pseudonyms. Bill begins by asking Rylee, the student who found the first quote, to begin by answering the questions about the quote she had selected.

Rylee explains that this quote comes near the beginning of the book, just after Joseph's family has been told about how Joseph disobeyed the laws of society (by assaulting a teacher and committing an act that fits the definition of statutory rape). Jack's family responds with compassion and hospitality, obeying their own rules for how to respond to someone in need. They agree to take Joseph as a foster child into their family.

The scene with the quote, Rylee explains, happens when Joseph arrives a couple of days later, and it is clear that he no longer obeys any rules of hospitality, if he ever did. He doesn't speak when Mrs. Stroud drops him off. He won't let Jack's mother hug him and won't shake hands with Jack's father. Jack brings him up to their room and Joseph climbs into the upper bunk without saying a word. But then Jack's dad calls them to come help with the milking.

Jack, as narrator, relates how they feed the cows and horses and then go to where the cows are tied up to milk. Jack's dad asks Joseph if he would like to try milking Rosie and explains that she is gentle. Joseph shakes his head. When they are almost done with the milking, though, Joseph rubs the end of Rosie's back. Rosie moos and sways back and forth. Jack tries to tell Joseph that means Rosie likes him, but Joseph cuts Jack off, says he doesn't care, and leaves the barn.

The next morning, when Joseph tries unsuccessfully to milk Rosie, she kicks over the pail. At that moment, Jack's father walks into the barn. He looks at Joseph and this spilled milk and then tells Joseph that he figures Joseph needs to finish what he started (p. 7).

Joseph points out that if Jack's dad really needs milk this desperately, he can go to a store like regular people do. One might expect Jack's dad to deal harshly with this disrespect, but he responds by saying that it isn't that the family needs the milk, it is that Rosie needs Joseph to milk her.

Joseph says that she doesn't need him to—but then Jack's father cuts him off, saying again that Rosie needs him (p. 7). Then Jack's father sits down and has Joseph sit next to him and he patiently shows Joseph how to milk Rosie. It takes Joseph several times to get the hang of it, but Jack's dad is patient. Joseph is finally successful.

In the classroom, Bill, the teacher, asks Rylee what the passage reminds her of, or how it connects to her. Rylee speaks of how, when she read the passage, she thought about her manager at work, who orders people to do tasks, but never shows the kind of wisdom that Jack's father shows here. Bill follows up, asking what it is about Jack's father that seems so wise.

Rylee explains that Jack's dad is neither strict nor unreasonable. Joseph is given time to learn and time to work out his own internal struggles as he does so. Obedience, then, is not responding to a merciless set of demands, like her manager makes, but a fluid obligation which Joseph will work his way into. And what he is being asked to do is not painful or difficult, but in fact, rewarding. Also, Jack's dad does the work alongside them.

Bill then opens up the discussion to the whole class by asking what thoughts or ideas this passage causes them to think. Daniel responds that obedience in this family is a matter of helping alongside, not following orders while authority figures enjoy the free labor. In fact, Jack's dad doesn't ever seem to exercise authority by yelling, demanding, or being physically threatening.

Bill broadens the prompt. He asks the students if there is any other idea that they can connect to this passage? Do they have any other insights?

Roland chimes in, saying that the scene that was mentioned looks less like the obeying that he grew up with, which was more a matter of his parents commanding him. He says this scene looks less like obedience and more like teaching, or maybe nurture.

Nadia suggests that maybe Joseph has not had a parent figure who has been patient and nurturing with him (a fact that will be confirmed later in the book).

OBEDIENCE TO FORCE

Bill can sense that the insights for this quote may be waning, and suggests the class move on to the next quote. It is worth noting, however, that the discussion which began the class, in which the students had remarkable insights about the whole entirety of the book, was focused on a single, one-sentence quote from the book. Zeroing in on small parts of the book allows students to stay anchored in the text and at the same time stretch out their insights over the whole book.

Bill reminds the class of the second sentence, where Joseph's dad implies that Jack is being forced to do chores (p. 30). Bill asks Robin, who volunteered that line, what the context of the quote was. Robin explains that the scene the quote comes from is a moment when Jack is heading out to the barn to milk the cows and sees a stranger standing there. Jack knows immediately that it is Joseph's dad. The stranger asks whether Joe is around. Jack notices that the cows are mooing the way they do when they perceive something to be anxious about. Jack tells Joseph's dad that Joseph is not around. Joseph's dad replies with the phrase the class is focusing on.

Bill asks Robin what the quote reminds them of, or how it connects to their life. The student says that the latter half of the quote, where Joseph's father asks Jack what he is here for, reminds them of times when they felt excluded—like something that somebody might say when you sit down at the wrong lunch table.

Bill then asks Robin what the quote causes them to think. Robin says they think that Joseph's dad is making some pretty big assumptions. One is that he assumes that the chores that Jack is doing are something he would not want to do without being made to. Joseph's dad also assumes that living in a foster home is some kind of punishment, like prison.

Several other students have their hands up, so Bill opens up the discussion. Harry points out that Jack's response when the stranger asks what he is doing here is to explain that this is his home (p. 31). And this response really goes against Joseph's father's assumption that a foster home must be like a prison.

And maybe for Jack, it also explains the first half of Joseph's father's statement, that chores are just a part of living.

Geni wants to follow the scene a bit further. She points out that just after that exchange, Jack's father arrives on the scene, setting down the milk pails and calming the cows. He asks the man if he is Joseph's father. The man says he is.

Then Jack's dad tells him he isn't allowed to visit.

Joseph's father says that he is visiting to see what kind of a "hellhole" the social services people have placed his son in (p. 31).

Geni points out that it seems clear that Joseph's father does not himself obey the rules—either of the state, since he has violated the law by visiting his son's foster care house—nor of politeness, since he has just called Jack's father's home a "hellhole." She goes on to point out one more part of the scene, where Joseph's father pushes on to accuse Jack's father of fostering children so they can shovel manure and do other barnyard tasks for him.

Jack's father responds by taking off his glasses and rubbing his eyes, then he tells Joseph's dad that they are caring for Joseph well, and that the time has come for Joseph's father to leave.

Geni doesn't really have a comment on this addition, but her friend Marcus jumps in. He points out that Joseph's father appears at first glance to be somebody who doesn't obey anything. In fact, however, he does leave in the end. Whether he leaves because he is reluctantly aware that he has to obey the law, or whether he obeys another law—the law of the bully, in which when he comes up against someone that he is unable to intimidate, he backs down—is not clear. But it is clear that, in spite of his bluster, Joseph's father does obey something.

Robin raises their hand to point out the contrast between this passage and the earlier one. Jack's father gets Joseph to obey by explaining things clearly, pointing out that the cow needs Joseph, and asking Joseph to do things rather than using force. Joseph's father, whether he is obeying the law or Jack's dad's firm voice, is still responding to the force behind the law, not obeying the law because he thinks it is the right thing to do.

While the discussion is still engaging students' interests, Bill moves on to the third quote: in which Joseph's father tells Joseph that the family is only taking him in for the money they get from the state for doing so (p. 128). Bill asks Megan to give the context of the quote she nominated.

Megan explains that Jack is coming back to the house from the barn where he has been doing his chores and he hears Joseph's father's voice. He comes into the living room in the middle of a conversation. Joseph's father, Mr. Brook, is saying that he has rights to see his own son and asks Jack's dad who he thinks he is by keeping Joseph from him (p. 128).

Mrs. Stroud responds firmly, warning Joseph's father that if he does not leave soon—but then leaving the threat unstated.

But Mr. Brook does not obey her request or pay any attention to her threat. He takes a step or two toward Jack's father and accuses him of pocketing the support money from the state. That is where the quote falls (p. 128).

Bill then asks Megan how the scene connects to her life. Megan says that her boss is always trying to lure people into working more shifts by offering them an extra ten dollars, or threatening people that if they keep coming late, he'll dock their pay. Megan says her boss thinks that the key to controlling everybody lies in money—that people will do whatever you want them to if you just give them a little extra cash. But Megan says that she has always thought there is a lot in life that is way more important than money—but that she figures Joseph's dad is like her boss—he thinks that the only reason anybody would do anything is because of money.

Bill then opens the discussion up to everybody and asks them what this scene causes them to think. Bess suggests that essentially this scene is a conflict of obedience with Joseph in the middle. Joseph's dad, Mr. Brook, is trying to get Joseph to obey him. In the beginning of the scene, Mr. Brook asserts his right to his son's obedience as if Joseph is a possession being stolen from him. He doesn't care about whether or not Joseph is okay, but who will control him. Bess reminds the class that a page or two before the scene, we found out that Mr. Brook wants to use Joseph's parental rights to Jupiter as a way to extract money from Madeleine's parents.

For Mr. Brook, this is about getting Joseph (or Jack's parents) to obey him, and relinquish Joseph, so that Mr. Brook can gain financially. And Bess says Mr. Brook tries to gain that obedience through threats, intimidation, and insults. She agrees with Megan's comment from before, that Mr. Brook understands obedience to only one thing, it seems—whatever will get him money. It is clear that he cannot imagine anyone caring for someone else's child for any reason other than money.

Gary points out that just after that scene, Jack's father first affirms what Mr. Brook is saying. They do, in fact, get payments from the state. Then Jack's father shows Joseph a drawer with records of all the state's payments and a bankbook in Joseph's name with the total amount the state has given them in it that Jack's mother explains is the start of Joseph's college fund.

Mr. Brook scoffs, saying that Joseph isn't going to go to college because if he went he would put on airs as if he knows everything—as if he were smarter than his dad. Gary points out that Joseph can certainly hear the same things that we can—namely that Mr. Brook is again trying to win Joseph's obedience through attacking what he values and reminding him what he heard growing up, that college is not for him.

Another student, Will, wonders if we might be able to see Mr. Brook, charitably, as a sympathetic character. The Department of Health and Human Services did take his son away. Maybe he does care for Joseph. He does promise Joseph a new life. This is a reference to the legal action that he needs Joseph for—in order to extract from Madeleine's parents a substantial amount of money. That money could change everything for them. Maybe Joseph's father would be a better father if he wasn't always trying to make ends meet.

Megan jumps back in. She says the whole thing is just a plea for Joseph to obey. But it comes with a veiled and frightening threat. If Joseph ever commands his father to do something again, the implication is there will be physical violence—perhaps the reason Joseph was taken away from his father in the first place. Finally, Mr. Brook wants Joseph to obey Mr. Brook's vision for Joseph—namely a life free of the drudgery and debilitating effects of going to college. Mr. Brook doesn't consider that Joseph might want to do something else with his life—like raise his daughter and go to college rather than escape it.

Bill, with one eye on the clock, summarizes the discussion before the bell rings. The class, he says, has uncovered differences in the purpose of obeying. While both Mr. Brook and Jack's parents would argue that they want the best for Joseph, Mr. Brooks definition of the best for Joseph starts with Joseph signing the legal document that would give away Joseph's rights to his child forever (obviously contrary to what Joseph would want to do). Then, Mr. Brook might argue, Joseph would be the beneficiary of Mr. Brook's newfound wealth (although most readers understand that Mr. Brook would control that money.)

Mr. Brook might be acting for Joseph's good, but his own good comes first and Joseph doesn't have any say in what happens. On the other hand, we have seen that with Jack's parents, Joseph has learned some obedience (milking Rosie and participating in the life of a family) without force and is also in a community where he has room (and structure) to grow and flourish. He concludes with some reminders about what is due and tells them that tomorrow, they will get a chance to talk about *The Beast Player*.

OBEDIENCE AND DUTY IN UEHASHI'S *THE BEAST PLAYER*

While *Orbiting Jupiter* is a realistic fiction novel set in contemporary North America, *The Beast Player* by Nahoko Uehashi is a traditional fantasy novel set in another world (though many aspects of its culture seem to resemble historical periods in Japan). How can a fantasy novel function as a prayer of obedience, when the setting and story do not even take place in our world? Cath Filmer-Davies argues that

> The existence of God in fantasy literature, then, does not depend upon the *Weltanschauung* of the author, who might create an apparently atheistic world, but rather upon a sense of presence that breaks through absence in matters of morality and judgment, mercy and compassion, forgiveness and reconciliation, kindness and comfort, depending upon the needs of the characters and the demands of the narrative itself. (1997, p. 73)

We can take Filmer-Davies's argument here and broaden it to argue that a prayer of obedience (or anything else) need not directly reference a deity, but may nonetheless function as a prayer to the extent that, as Filmer-Davies says, the work allows a presence to break through the absence. In the case of *The Beast Player*, Uehashi is addressing a moral conflict between an obedience of culture or societal rules, and a personal knowledge of rightness and wrongness on the part of the characters of the book.

And so, the development of the theme of obedience is much different in the two books. Bill wanted to see whether his class would see those differences. After assigning the class to read *The Beast Player*, Bill used havruta once again to explore what they noticed in their reading.

The Beast Player was originally copyrighted in Japan as a novel in 2009 (after a successful run as a manga—a type of graphic novel). It was also adapted into a popular anime which ran in Japan in 2009—but it wasn't translated into English and published in novel form until 2019.

As we mentioned briefly at the beginning of this chapter, the story concerns Elin, whose mother, Sohyon, cares for the Toda, powerful and ferocious water beasts that are an important part of her kingdom's defenses. Several Toda die one night and Sohyon investigates. When she is blamed for the deaths of the beasts and sentenced to death herself, Sohyon does not protest. Elin tries to rescue her mom, but instead, Sohyon puts her on the back of a Toda and commands the beast to take Elin far away to a distant kingdom..

An exiled teacher turned beekeeper named Joeun finds Elin on the beach, exhausted and barely alive. He nurses her back to health and raises her as his own daughter. Eventually Elin enters a school for those who care for the beasts of the Yojeh, the ruler of the kingdom. Unlike the Toda, these beasts are land-based and have wings. Eventually, Elin's skill in healing and caring for the beasts puts her in the center of an internal power grab among the ruling class and also an external threat to the kingdom from an army of rebels.

Again, Bill starts by asking his students if each of them can come up with a sentence or moment from the book that took their attention—preferably a moment connected to the theme of obedience. Once the students have made their selections, Bill types them on the white board and they narrow down the list of nominees to those that have the most potential for discussion. Students pick four sentences:

> First, a sentence from the beginning of the book in which Sohyon tells Elin that Sohyon's mother taught her that the most important thing was the Oath—and that it was more important than her own survival, or the survival of her family (p. 14).
> Second, Joeun's warning to Elin to stay away from the box that contains the beehive (p. 47).
> Third, a sentence that is a warning from one of Elin's teachers to a class of students who will one day care for the royal beasts—that students must never approach a beast without being fully alert and prepared for anything (p. 124).
> And finally, the correction offered from one of the royal guards to another that there is never a time when they are not on duty (p. 82).

As before, Bill arranges the sentences in the order they appear in the book. Then he starts with the first sentence on the white board, asking Joni, who nominated it, to read it aloud. Then he asks Joni to explain the context for that sentence.

Joni describes this scene in which Elin's mother Sohyon explains that even the name of Elin's ethnic culture, the Ao-Loh, means oath-guardian or oath-protector. Her people swore an oath to prevent a terrible mistake from long ago from being repeated. Then comes Sohyon's reminder that keeping the Oath is more important than staying alive or even protecting one's family (p. 14).

When Elin asks what the great mistake was, Sohyon is silent for a long time, then finally explains that it was a disaster and a flagrant breaking of the Oath that brought their society to the brink of dying out. She says that her ancestors promised that such a disaster would never happen again and they became nomads living in the wild, serving neither the True Ruler (the Yojeh), nor the Grand Duke. Ever since then, her people, the Ao-Loh, are taught strictly to follow the law of the Oath. They may not marry anyone who is not a Ao-Loh and must never put down roots in one place, but must keep wandering (pp. 14–15). Sohyon goes on to confess that by marrying Elin's father and settling down in the village, Sohyon has broken the Oath.

Bill asks Joni if this reminds her of anything. Joni says it doesn't, because she can't imagine anybody agreeing to give up the right to choose who to spend her life with or where to live because of an oath. She says she could imagine somebody being forced to follow those rules in Afghanistan with the Taliban, but not in her world.

Now that students have time to consider the passage, Bill opens it up to the whole class and asks them how this passage connects to them, and what it causes them to think.

Brian says that the idea isn't that unreasonable. He says that we find out later in the book that the rules make sense. Just before that scene, for example, Sohyon is not forbidding Elin to talk about what she noticed about the dead Toda merely out of concern for her safety—though that may be a part of it—but because the truth about the Toda is a matter of protecting the Toda and humans and preventing a bloody war. So obedience here—keeping the secret—is not a matter of gaining power or personal gain but rather a matter of responsibility to the greater good, to society, and to protecting the peace.

Jacques agrees, pointing out that Sohyon did not disobey another person over a question of force and free will, she disobeyed a societal law and brought a potential consequence against all people into being.

Frances fires back that Sohyon was about to be killed for the deaths of the Toda which she did not cause—and that in dying, she would be dooming her daughter to living as an outcast orphan.

Kathryn agrees, pointing out that later in the scene, the Chief Inspector, who has been called in to investigate the death of the Toda, has an argument with the Chief Steward, who is both Sohyon's father-in-law and the supervisor of her work. When the Chief Steward defends Sohyon, claiming she has outstanding skill as a healer, the Inspector reminds the Chief Steward that the most important qualification for a Toda caregiver is being completely loyal to the Ao-Loh, the kingdom in which they live (p. 17).

Jacques suggests that the most important qualification for a Toda caregiver ought to be that the person does a good job caring for the Toda.

Bill jumps in to remind the students that not only is this a fantasy novel, about a culture different from the one we live in, but it is also a novel written in the context of contemporary Japanese culture, which also holds different values than contemporary North American culture. So maybe the class ought to reframe the question not so much as one of whether the society in *The Beast Player* has good values, but how individual characters respond to those values.

After a pause, Gary observes that Sohyon is caught between obeying the laws and rules of the society she now serves and obeying the laws of her own people. What makes the moral dilemma even more difficult is that if she fails to uphold the secrets of her people, that will bring about war and death and great suffering to the beasts in her care. On the other hand, if she keeps her people's secret—and lies about what she knows about why the Toda died— she herself will likely be sentenced to death and her daughter Elin will be left without a mother and will be branded the child of a traitor.

Joni points out that while there are some differences, *The Beast Player* does resemble *Orbiting Jupiter* because both books at some point put obeying the deep bond between parent and child up against something else. In *Orbiting Jupiter,* Joseph must decide between his obligation to obey his foster family, to obey the threats of his father, or to obey his own need and responsibility to be with his daughter. In *The Beast Player*, Sohyon weighs the responsibility to obey her oath against the need to obey her responsibility, love, and obligation to her child.

Bill suggests that the next sentence on the board may give them more to think about. He asks Kristin, who found the sentence, to read it and provide the context for it.

Kristin reads the sentence which warns Elin not to go near the beehive box (p. 47). Kristin then explains that this takes place after Elin escapes on the back of a Toda, and the old schoolteacher Joeun takes her in and gives her many instructions to obey. Elin's curiosity gets the better of her, however, and she gets too close to one of his beehives. She is startled when a hand grabs her, covers her mouth, and carries her all the way to the house. Joeun then warns her to stay away from the beehives. Elin apologizes.

Joeun goes on to explain that his honeybees almost never sting anybody, but if they are threatened, they will sacrifice themselves to defend their hive. Elin apologizes again. Then Joeun relaxes and explains that she gave him quite a scare.

Bill asks Kristin if the passage she read reminds her of anything. Kristin recalls the moment in *Orbiting Jupiter* when Jack's father responds calmly to Joseph's sarcastic remark about how the family should just get their milk from a grocery store. Kristin points out that, like Jack's dad, Joeun is making rules not to assert power, but to help Elin. In this case, it is to help her be safe. Kristin adds that, like Jack's dad, Joeun is gentle in correcting her and gives an explanation of why he made the rule.

Bill opens the discussion to the rest of the class, asking them how the passage connects to them, or to other moments in the story. Pauly says that the passage is maybe the only moment when Joeun speaks strongly to Elin. He does not assert his power over her, or to get her to do his bidding, but he is concerned for her safety.

Curtis, knowing that the class was going to focus on obedience, has made a list of Joeun's rules. He points out that these are not commands to do chores, but mostly they are related to her safety. He warns her to wear a hat and gloves when they work with the beehives (p. 40); to hand him the sprayer to control the bees (p. 43); not to come too near to the bees (p. 45); to stay away from the bee box (p. 46), and not to crawl under the horse (p. 65–66).

Frances agrees, but points out that in their discussion so far, it is still possible to identify a major difference between the way that obedience works in the two books. Frances argues that obedience to someone you love looks mostly the same in the two books, but the other category, obedience to something outside a love relationship involves individual power and force in *Orbiting Jupiter* and involves more societal pressure or responsibility in the case of *The Beast Player*.

Brenna reminds everyone that in *Beast Player*, Elin starts out learning to obey people she loves, like Joeun or Esalu, but then later she has to decide whether to obey the Yojeh and her representatives, or her mother's people. And while Elin may respect the laws and traditions, she does not really respect those who are commanding her.

Bill asks if anyone else has any other insights, then realizes that discussion in response to this quote has run out so he asks Teri, who suggested the third quote, to give the class the context for that quote.

Teri points out that the quote about the students being careful to stay on their guard around the beasts (p. 124) raises the stakes of obeying or not obeying considerably. Elin is now a student in the school for caretakers of the Royal Beasts. Teri points out that the teachers give the students many warnings, explaining that beasts seem quiet and peaceful when they are not threatened or excited, but that they are vicious when threatened or excited. Teri says the warning reminds her of Joeun's warning about the bees, and concludes that the teachers' commands, like Joeun's, ensure students' safety—but instead of a bee sting or two, disobedience of the teachers' rules could cost a limb, or even their lives.

Bill asks Teri what it reminds her of, or what it causes her to draw a connection to. Teri says it reminds her of orcas. She says she did a report on orcas when she was in grade school and read about how orcas are sometimes called killer whales and thought about how that doesn't make sense. They do eat seals and fish, but a lot of animals eat other animals. Calling them killer whales makes us see them only as powerful killers. Teri says that the rules at Elin's school encourage her fellow students to think of the beasts only as bloodthirsty killers.

While they are powerful animals, Elin later realizes there is more to the beasts than just viciousness. They are also intelligent and can be loyal and caring as well. Teri suggests that the way the teachers passed on commands for the safety of their students, may have also passed on a way of looking at the beasts, which limited how the students could see the beasts.

Ryan raises his hand. He points out that when Elin first meets the young beast Leelan, who was wounded during an assassination attempt on the life of the Yojeh, she empathizes with its loneliness and pain and is reprimanded by Esalu who understands her pity but warns her against getting emotionally connected to the beast. Doing so, he says, will make it difficult for her to stay objective when making difficult decisions and protecting herself. This is so important that Esalu reconsiders her decision to ask Elin to observe Leelan (p. 135).

Ryan says this backs up what Teri said. It is clear that rules made to protect the students (and the teachers) from the beasts have resulted in a cold and clinical view of them, which we later find out limits Esalu and other's ability to help Leelan. It is Elin's empathy that helps her to see how to restructure the pen to set Leelan at ease and eventually heal her.

Bill asks if anyone else has any thoughts about this. Naomi raises her hand. She says that in order to heal Leelan, Elin has to see Leelan as more than a dangerous animal, she has to see Leelan as a child who misses its mother. Then Elin has to decide whether to disobey the safety commands repeatedly. Her success with Leelan seems to vindicate this choice and may remind readers that not all obedience is wise, even if the commands are for Elin's own good.

Lisa has noticed a similar theme in the Harry Potter books, when Harry and his friends often have to decide to break the rules of the school for the greater good of the students or even the wizarding world in general.

Bill sees that the time is growing short and decides to skip to the final quote. He asks Eli, who suggested that quote, to read it and, like the others, provide the context for the quote.

Eli starts with the quote about how the royal bodyguards are never off duty (p. 82), then explains that another way obedience comes up in this book is in terms of another character, Ialu, one of the Se Zan. Eli explains that the Se Zan are living shields, and their job is to protect the Yojeh at all costs. In order that they not be swayed by any outside influences that might threaten their loyalty, the Se Zan are not allowed to marry. Like many Se Zan, Ialu was selected for service when he was a young boy and his family was paid a large amount of money when he was taken away. Ialu and other Se Zan have sacrificed relationships and family and are prepared to sacrifice their lives to protect their nation's ruler.

Eli goes on to explain the quote is taken from a scene between Kailu, another Se Zan, and Ialu. When Kailu and Ialu walk past a group of older drunken men cursing and kicking a young man, Kailu accuses Ialu of being cold and lacking compassion. Ialu doesn't respond at first, and so Kailu turns toward the young man being abused and says with disgust that he doesn't need Ialu's help anyway. Ialu tells him to ignore the situation. Kailu says that he is not on duty and warns Ialu not to try to stop him. Ialu's response is short, He tells Kailu that they are never off duty.

As they walk away from the young man, Kailu complains to Ialu that the life they lead is miserable. Ialu responds quietly that if Kailu doesn't like the life they lead, he should renounce his vow and quit. Ialu insists that it is impossible to do the work that their lives are dedicated to if they have any doubt about it (p. 82).

Bill asks Eli if this reminds him of anything, or if he can connect it to something outside the book. Eli says it is obviously like the Secret Service with the president of the United States, and how when the president is giving a speech or whatever, they don't listen to what he is saying because they are scanning the crowd looking for threats.

Bill then opens the discussion up to everyone again. Kristin raises her hand and says that this is a strange kind of obedience because the Se Zan don't usually seem to have any specific orders other than eliminating threats to the Yojeh's life. They obey the focus of their larger calling more than they obey any person. The nature of their obedience resembles that of Elin's mother—committed to principles and loyalty more than to direct obedience to a person or responding to the threat of force or law.

Eli raises his hand. He sees a parallel between the life of a Se Zan, which is a life of complete obedience to the all-encompassing task of keeping the Yojeh safe, and the way that those who care for the Royal Beasts are bound to the Royal Beast Canon. He remembers reading that the beasts are a symbol of the Yojeh's sovereignty, and when humans are caring for the beasts, they must follow the Beast Canon completely. Every action the keepers take must be noted, from what the beasts eat to the type of straw used for bedding in their stalls (pp. 172–73).

Eli says that while the Se Zan follow an oath and instructions that do not seem to be written down, and the Royal Beast keepers follow a written Canon, the reverence for the law they follow is similarly deep and unwavering.

After a pause in which Bill waits for the next student to speak, Jenne points out that it would be wrong to think that people in the world of *The Beast Player* follow these laws blindly. The main conflict in *The Beast Player* occurs when the law runs up against the safety of the Yojeh (in the case of the Se Zan) or the safety of the Royal Beasts (in the case of the keepers.).

Joni says there is a difference in the way individuals respond to the law in the two different books. It is hard to imagine in *Orbiting Jupiter*, Jack's dad begging Joseph's dad to return to the shelter that the law offers. Joni says this is a big difference between the way obedience is treated in the two books. In *Orbiting Jupiter*, the law is a constraint, imposed from outside of the person affected, and the law is an impediment, something to be reluctantly obeyed or, if no authority is present, to be flagrantly disobeyed. In that book, Jack's family offers an alternative, in which obedience arises out of gratitude and love, not out of power.

But in *The Beast Player*, Joni says, the law can function as a shelter. It can be a thing that protects and keeps communities safe from themselves. It protects individuals, but also groups. It protects and preserves a way of life. And if laws are broken, the repercussions reach far beyond individuals to include the survival of cultures.

David mentions that we are missing one of the most important relationships to obedience in the book: Elin's relationship with Leelan, the Royal Beast. For most of the book, it is a relationship based on mutual respect. Elin doesn't so much command Leelan as request that the beast do things and Leelan doesn't so much obey as take actions to help Elin. Toward the end of the book, however, that relationship changes. After Leelan wounds Elin, she is forced to use the silent whistle. From that moment, their relationship changes from one of mutual respect to one that is based on a power struggle.

Bill jumps in to say that with that shift comes a redefinition of what it means for Leelan to obey. Where previously obedience was followed by a stronger sense of connection between Elin and Leelan, now, after this power confrontation, it is likely that Leelan feels some resentment from being forced to obey (even though cleaning her stall will benefit her). While there will still be moments of cooperation between the two, the threat of the whistle will always be there.

Bill then points out that time is almost up. He thanks the students for participating well and summarizes the discussion by saying that while there are aspects of the cultural obedience described in *The Beast Player*, that might seem nobler somehow that the individualistic obedience described in *Orbiting Jupiter*; in fact, the community-based, culturally grounded law can be misused in a selfish manner as well.

Both books the class has discussed, *Orbiting Jupiter* and *The Beast Player*, have plenty of material to lead to strong and deep discussions of the way in which both books function as prayers of obedience. And using havruta (or any of the other approaches discussed in this book) not only opens up discussion, but keeps that discussion focused on the text, allowing students to move from a single sentence to the theme that moves through the whole book.

Chapter 9

Prayers of Contemplation in *Where the Mountain Meets the Moon*

Human beings have a long history of contemplation, turning the mind inward or focusing the mind on a particular object, thought, or activity to train attention and awareness to solve problems, understand something deeply, or create a sense of calm and inner harmony. Contemplation plays a part in many different religious traditions including studying scriptures, praying, and meditating.

Christian contemplation sometimes takes the form of a meditation prayer in which a structured attempt is made to get in touch with and deliberately reflect upon the revelations of God. Buddhists pursue meditative contemplation as part of the path toward awakening and nirvana. In Hinduism, contemplative meditation occurs when, "having become calm and concentrated, one perceives the self within oneself" (Flood, 1996).

Today, contemplation is practiced in various ways in cultures all over the world, though more often the focus is less about faith and more about altering consciousness, finding awareness, and achieving peace. Many things can inspire contemplation. Larsen (2017) writes that remembrance of a moving pastoral scene allows William Wordsworth to still his mind and see into the life of things (p. 137); flowers and dough serve as a pathway to contemplation for Margret Silf (p. 136); and that nature (p. 136) as well as innovative shots in movies (p. 138) can draw Larsen into a contemplative and tranquil state.

One type of contemplation is meditation. While not all contemplation is meditation and not all meditation is contemplation, the two terms do overlap. The website Healthline distinguishes between nine types of popular contemplative meditation.

1. In *mindfulness meditation*, people pay attention to their thoughts as they pass through their mind. They do not judge the thoughts or become involved with them. They simply observe and take note of any patterns.

2. In *spiritual meditation*, people seek a deeper connection with their god or with the universe.
3. *Focused meditation* uses any of the five senses or external influences to help focus their attention.
4. *Movement meditation* is an active form of meditation where the movement such as walking, gardening, yoga, or other activities guide people.
5. In *mantra meditation*, people use a repetitive sound, word, phrase to experience deeper levels of awareness.
6. *Transcendental meditation* uses a series of words that are specific to each practitioner to focus the mind for contemplation.
7. *Progressive relaxation* involves slowly tightening and relaxing one muscle group at a time throughout the body.
8. *Love-kindness meditation* strengthens feelings of compassion, kindness, and acceptance toward oneself and others. It typically involves opening the mind to receive love from others and then sending a series of well wishes to loved ones, friends, acquaintances, and all living beings.
9. In *visualization meditation*, practitioners visualize positive scenes or images to enhance feelings of relaxation, peace, and calmness. Alternatively, they can imagine themselves succeeding at specific goals, which is intended to increase focus and motivation.

These meditation practices can characterize contemplation in real life, but also in fiction. *Where the Mountain Meets the Moon*, an adolescent novel by Grace Lin, is an example of a novel which functions as a prayer of contemplation. The book tells the tale of Minli, a courageous young Chinese girl. She is aware of her family's poverty and parents' eagerness to change their fortune, and is inspired by the stories her dad tells her every night, so she starts a quest for a prosperous future for them all. She encounters various people and makes new friends along the journey, who help her overcome the hurdles to her goal.

Where the Mountain Meets the Moon showcases different types of contemplation practiced by Minli and other characters depicted in the novel. The sacred text reading practice of marginalia can allow student readers to see how the theme of meditation shapes characters, and reinforces the theme throughout the book, and can open the floor up for vigorous discussion.

WHERE THE MOUNTAIN MEETS THE MOON

Where the Mountain Meets the Moon won the Newbery Medal in 2010. Grace Lin is the author of many other books, including picture books, elementary level books, and two sequels to *Where the Mountain Meets the Moon*: *Starry River of the Sky* (2012) and *When the Sea Turned to Silver* (2016).

Minli lives in Fruitless Mountain with her parents—Ba and Ma. The name of the village reflects their real life accurately, poor and difficult, but they love each other in a tangible way. Ba, Ma, and Minli work in the fields every day, but Ba and Ma always ask Minli to go home early so that she does not work for as long hours as Ba and Ma do; Ba and Ma always save food for Minli; Minli also cares for Ba and Ma so much that she makes every effort to change their life and make them not fret about money.

The name Minli means quick thinking, which resembles her lively and impulsive spirit. While Ba and Ma seem to seldom engage in reflection of any sort and passively accept their difficult fate, Minli is mindful of everything and everyone present in her life and gives attention to them. For example, stories, scenes, animals, and people all can draw her to engage in contemplation and reflection, which help her decide what choices to make and paths to take. We'll start by considering the different types of meditation Minli practices.

CONTEMPLATION OF SCRIPTURE

Minli is not religious, but the types of contemplation she practices are similar to scriptural contemplation and study techniques. In Christianity, Judaism, Islam, Buddhism, and the Hindu faith, worshipers contemplate the words of scriptures to develop a deeper attachment to faith and a clearer understanding of how the world works. Contemplating both scriptures and the events of one's life clarifies the meaning and significance of both. Focusing on a text can also internalize the words of the passage. When we pause in any reading and think for a moment about how what we read has meaning for our lives and for the world, the written word comes alive.

Dietrich Bonhoeffer, a German theologian, in *Life Together*, argues that even as one does not analyze the words of a person you love, but rather accept what they say to you, in a similar way, one's task with scripture is to accept it and ponder it in one's heart, as the Bible speaks of Mary doing. That, he says, is meditation (1939). He goes on to recommend spending a whole week on a single text, which shows it is important to resist passing over passages superficially.

Some Christian scholars argue that contemplation of scriptures is not enough, and Christians should also contemplate current events. Thomas Merton suggests that anyone who has contemplated the Passion of Christ but has not contemplated the genocide that occurred in Dachau, Auschwitz, and other concentration camps had not really experienced what it means to be a

Christian (Foster, 1978). Contemplation upon current events is a way to ask God for prophetic insight to discern where things lead and ask for guidance in how to respond.

The two forms of Christian contemplation, focusing on connections between the text and the world, and connecting the text and one's personal life, deeply resemble Minli's practice, although she does not identify as Christian.

Minli ponders the story of Fruitless Mountain and the story of the Old Man of the Moon. Ba tells the story of the Fruitless Mountain which explains why the mountain is bare and the land around it is hard and the river is dark. All these are the result of the sorrow and grief of Jade Dragon, whose four children sacrificed themselves by turning themselves into rivers in order to help humans suffering from drought and death because of Jade Dragon's curse. Jade Dragon turns herself into a river in hopes of being reunited with her children, but the children's spirits have been released and they are not in the river, and the mountain yields nothing.

With each story that Ba tells, Minli imagines how wonderful it would be if the mountain once more was covered with blooms and fruit trees. She imagines how prosperous her village would be then (p. 9). The question Minli contemplates is how Fruitless Mountain could ever grow green again. She also wonders how she could help bring fortune to her home.

These questions are deeply connected. If Minli's family did not live in the region of Fruitless Mountain, or if the mountain were not bare, her Ba and Ma's hard work would pay off and the entire family could have more resources than they do now, and Ma would not sigh relentlessly. Minli contemplates the story in this context, and the story speaks to her and deepens her understanding on her life and motivates her to search for change.

The Old Man of the Moon is another story that Minli has heard multiple times and has ruminated on. After listening to the story of Fruitless Mountain, Minli often asks questions and Ba always responds the same way: by telling her that to find the answer to that question, she will have to ask the Old Man of the Moon. The story goes that the Old Man of the Moon is the guardian of the Book of Fortune which holds all the knowledge of the world—the past, present, and future—and he is the only person who can read the book and thereby answer any question in the world.

One day, Magistrate Tiger comes across the Old Man of the Moon who tells Magistrate Tiger that his son will marry a grocer's daughter in the future, which goes against Magistrate Tiger's coveted wish of being of royal blood, so he demands that the grocer's daughter should be killed in order to realize his dream. Many years later, however, his son ends up marrying one of the emperor's many granddaughters, who turns out to be a grocer's daughter adopted by the king of the city.

Each time Ba tells the story, Minli points out that the Old Man of the Moon was right. Each time Minli hears the story she is more determined to ask the Old Man of the Moon how to bring fortune to her home. Her contemplation of the story gives her determination as well as insight. At the same time, her contemplation clarifies for her that her priority is to find the Old Man of the Moon.

In addition to the stories Minli contemplates, she carefully observes and reflects on what she observes in life. Ba and Ma's hard work each day from the dawn to dusk, Ma's constant sigh, the scarcity of food and other daily necessities make her consider how to change their lives and bring fortune to their home. For example, early in the book we read that on a night when Minli had trouble sleeping, she lies awake listening to the echo of Ma's words and when she shuts her eyes, she sees Ba's hand, trembling from working hard, giving food to the goldfish (p. 23). What Minli has seen in life draws her attention, and she spends time reflecting on it.

Minli's meditation on stories and events of her time bears a resemblance to religious contemplation and gives her insight, guidance, and determination in her circumstances.

MOVEMENT MEDITATION

Movement meditation is an active form of contemplation where physical movement such as walking, gardening, or yoga guides people in their reflection. Minli practices this kind of contemplation as she travels from her hometown to Never-Ending Mountain. She encounters different things and people along the journey, all of which cause her to reflect thoughtfully. She contemplates her meetings with the dragon, the buffalo boy, Da-A-Fu's family, and Wu Kang.

The dragon is the first adventure for Minli. The dragon tells his own story. Originally, the dragon was a painting by Master Chen to cover his village's required tribute to Magistrate Tiger. Chen painted the dragon on the ground, not flying in the sky like all other dragons, so that Magistrate Tiger could see how his wealth weighs him down. Magistrate Tiger realized that the dragon did not have eyes and ordered his servant to paint in the eyes. The dragon then became alive and fled Magistrate Tiger's mansion, destroying it in the process. The dragon has lived in the forest ever since. When Minli meets him he is tied up and crying in the lake.

At the beginning of her story, Minli is still learning how to contemplate and understand stories. Her focus is very much on her parents' poverty. As the book continues, however, Minli becomes a more empathic listener and a more thoughtful learner. The dragon's loneliness in the forest, annoyance at being bullied by monkeys, and frustration in its inability to fly catches Minli's sympathy. Later, in response to Minli's care for the dragon, the dragon fights against a monster to save Minli so that he is injured severely. The dragon's genuine friendship and care for her causes Minli to consider what she can do for him.

Minli and the buffalo boy meet for the first time when she tries to get into the Inner City and see the king after arriving in the City of Bright Moonlight with the dragon. Minli learns from the buffalo boy that the Inner City is open to the public once a year, on the Moon Festival only, and this year's Moon Festival is gone, so it is more difficult for Minli to see the king. The buffalo boy invites Minli to his home since Minli has nowhere to stay. At the buffalo boy's place, Minli learns that he has been living alone with the buffalo in a small and meager home since his parents died a few years ago. Despite his poor life, the buffalo boy is content with the company of the buffalo and the sporadic visits of a mysterious girlfriend about whom he knows little but that she is his real friend.

The buffalo boy's living situation reminds Minli of her own family and home. Minli contemplates the two families and homes, and becomes aware of the difference between the buffalo boy and her own family. While both are poor, the buffalo boy is happy, while her own family is filled with bitterness.

After they leave the City of Bright Moonlight, the dragon is injured by a ferocious tiger while trying to protect Minli. Minli rushes to the nearby village for help. On the way to the village, she meets the twins, Da-A-Fu, who defeat the tiger by fooling him. Da-A-Fu's grandfather shows up to bring them home when the tiger dies, but he learns of the dragon's injury from Minli and gives the dragon medical treatment in a cave. While the dragon heals, Da-A-Fu take Minli back to their home and let her rest.

Minli gets to know Da-A-Fu's large family of grandparents, parents, uncles, aunts, and cousins and is impressed by their hospitality and unity. She is excited to learn that Da-A-Fu can bring them to Never-Ending Mountain. The dragon heals quickly with the help of the homemade medicine, and soon Minli, the dragon, and Da-A-Fu head out to Never-Ending Mountain together. Arriving there, they send a message to the Old Man of the Moon by flying a kite to him, which Minli thought of because of Da-A-Fu's ancestors' story.

Da-A-Fu's laughter as they run down the mountain gives Minli something to think about. Da-A-Fu's large family are not any better off than Minli's parents, as evidenced by the jacket they make for Minli using a patch from each person's clothes. Minli is puzzled at why they are content with life and do not want to change. Once again, she contemplates this while walking on her journey, and once again it is a form of movement meditation.

Minli eventually lands on the Never-Ending Mountain by walking on the red rope bridge. As a rabbit leads her to the Old Man of the Moon, Minli learns the story of Wu Kang who is chopping down the only tree there. Before coming to the Never-Ending Mountain, Wu Kang had a good life, surrounded by a beautiful wife, healthy children, loving family, and faithful friends and neighbors. However, he was discontent despite being skilled at many things, and despite his wife's plea that he be content with what he had, Wu Kang left his family and searched for an immortal master to satisfy his incessant dissatisfaction with what he had and his constant greed for more.

Eventually, he found the Old Man of the Moon who agreed (with some reservations) to teach him marvelous things. However, Wu Kang did not appreciate the wondrous lessons taught by the Old Man of the Moon. He still asked for more, which made the Old Man of the Moon aware of Wu Kang's impatience and discontentment and also what Wu Kang really needed to learn. Minli ponders Wu Kang's story while listening to it, and realizes Wu Kang's chopping makes the strange moon rain that Da-A-Fu's family's village is named after.

Minli practices movement meditation along her journey and benefits greatly from it. She contemplates the wisdom she has learned and applies that wisdom to both immediate problems and some larger questions of life. Contemplation also helps her connect what took place generations before with the challenges she faces in her life, including her quest after the solution to the problem her family faces.

LOVE-KINDNESS MEDITATION

Love-kindness meditation strengthens feelings of compassion, kindness, and acceptance toward oneself and others. It typically involves opening the mind to receive love from others and then sending a series of well-wishes to loved ones, friends, acquaintances, and all living beings. Ma's character evolution through the novel reveals the effectiveness of such contemplation.

Ma is hardworking but often begrudges the barren mountain and meager land she lives on. She sighs with resentment at poverty, and she thinks that stories Ba tells Minli only make her daydream. Ma often focuses solely on their bare house, meager rice supply, and complains that the only thing they have plenty of is stories. When Minli buys a goldfish using her money in the hope to bring fortune to their home, Ma lashes out at her purchase and complains that the fish will consume some of the little rice they have. She blames Ba for Minli's running away from home.

Ma begins to reflect on her behavior, her family, and the wealth she longs for while waiting for Minli to return home from her quest. She asks Ba to tell her the story of the dragon's pearl, and when Ba says that they are like the dragon waiting for a sign of his pearl, Ma speaks without the usual jealousy and covetousness that she usually has when she is talking about other people's wealth (p. 175). Years of bitterness and hardship are slowly being transformed to a sad serenity.

Ma's contemplative epiphany is revealed when she tells her own story based on their own life. She recounts to Ba what each member of the family has done and how each person approaches life differently. In so doing, she conveys her true remorse in terms of her own actions to the family. Her contemplation enables her to be aware of her own issues and extend love and kindness to her beloved people.

MARGINALIA

As we mentioned in chapter 7, marginalia are marks made in the margins of a book or other document. They may be scribbles, comments, glosses, critiques, doodles, or illuminations. Dr. Hannah McKillop briefly recounts the history and development of marginalia, focusing on the two phases of marginalia (2020). The two phases are divided by the printing revolution. Before the printing industry was well-developed, printed materials were limited and only available to the wealthy, so marginalia primarily consisted of textual collations and corrections, explanations of hard words and obscure passages, references to sources, and illustrative examples.

Marginal comments were originally used as a learning tool rather than a chance for readers to express their personal opinions of the text to themselves or the author. The leap of the printing industry in the sixteenth century brought more books so that more people began to write in book margins. It is safe to say that writers of marginalia are self-conscious readers. Writing margin notes forces readers to slow down, contemplate what they are reading, and interact with the text in new ways.

What sorts of things readers record in the margins of a book partly depends upon the genre of the book. McKillop points out that "generally fictional books tend to be less commonly annotated than other genres" (2020, n.p.). This may be because the story draws the reader in so quickly and so deeply. Annotating requires stepping out of the story from time to time and contemplating the connections, discoveries, and insights that the reader brings to the book and the book brings to the reader. So the act of consciously choosing to write in the margins of a YA novel allows for a different kind of engagement with the narrative.

The sacred reading practice of marginalia pairs well with YA novels of contemplation because it allows the reader to engage in contemplation even as the characters in the novel are. Marginal comments are the signs of readers' contemplation while they read the text.

The teacher could start by assigning students to consciously make marginal comments as they read, perhaps in response to a suggested theme. Once the students have read the book and made marginal comments (either with pencil or sticky notes), the teacher can start the discussion by asking students to select a marginal comment that they wrote that struck them as interesting (or that connects to the theme being discussed).

In one class, Ben, a student reader, raises his hand. He is struck by a line that describes how Jade Dragon's children came down to the earth and transformed into water, eventually saving the humans (p. 8). The teacher asks Ben what it is about that sentence that takes his attention. Ben says that beside that sentence in his book, he wrote, "Children sacrifice themselves and fight against injustice revealed by Mom."

Ben explains that Jade Dragon is a god in charge of clouds. She is angry to learn that people are tired of rain, so she retaliates by letting it never rain. Her four children are compassionate to humans and bold enough to stand with them. They know it is their mom's fault, but they think it is unjust and they are willing to sacrifice themselves to help humans suffering from drought be able to escape the unjust penalty their mother has levied against the humans.

Ben says that, after he thought about it some more, he wrote below his first annotation, "How does that make Jade Dragon feel? Prideful? Heartbroken?"

The teacher then asks the whole class what insights they can bring to Ben's comment. Asking this question makes room for the discussion to develop and deepen.

Lilli raises her hand and points out that the children of the Jade Dragon were trying to restore justice and that their mother was a force for unreasonable vengeance and retribution. So the children are really creatures of love and peace. She wonders aloud if there are other characters in the book that are either forces of retribution and injustice or love and peace. The teacher writes that on the board as a possible theme to explore later

Jon points out that in history class, they had read some of Martin Luther King's speeches and remembers a quote from King that he thinks applies to this passage. "Darkness cannot drive out darkness. Only light can do that. Hate cannot drive out hate. Only love can do that."

Miranda raises her hand with desperation. The teacher calls on her and Miranda says she underlined a sentence from later in the book that she thinks connects to this one. The sentence describes how Wu Kang was never satisfied (pp. 182–84). Miranda wrote in the margin by one of the sentences, "greed vs. contentment."

The teacher asks her to explain the connection that she is seeing. Miranda explains that Wu Kang's story shows that he is never content with what he has and always hopes to have more. She says this connects to the sentence that Ben read because Jade Dragon is a lot like Wu Kang. "Both of them are not satisfied. Wu Kang wants more possessions. Jade Dragon wants more humans to appreciate the work she does."

Ben jumps in, agreeing. He points out that it is okay for Wu Kang to have dreams, "but the problem is that Wu Kang doesn't have any patience and he doesn't spend any time trying to reach any of his dreams. He always wants the easy way out."

Sarwat picks up the thread from there. "Right. And since he never makes any progress toward any of his dreams, they never satisfy him. So, Wu Kang's discontentment is really more the result of his impatience than his greed."

At this point the teacher reminds students that the theme they are focusing on for this book is contemplation, and asks if anyone has any annotations that might connect the thread they have been discussing so far with the theme of contemplation. Several hands shoot up, and the discussion is off in a new direction.

ENDINGS

Where the Mountain Meets the Moon has many inspiring stories and characters who reflect about what they are hearing and what they are learning. As a prayer of contemplation, it is certainly rich with material. Many of our students live in a high-speed world, where work and life are often mashed together in a blur of activity. The pace of life seems to be getting faster and more frenetic every year. The illusion of productivity and high performance can take a toll on the quality of life.

Contemplation, by its very nature, takes our awareness into the field of the timeless. We experience our true nature as human beings by engaging in thought and reflection about what we read and discuss. Young adult readers can discover the value of contemplation as they read about how it helps to guide Minli in her quest.

Marginalia can be one the ways to practice meditation and contemplation. Readers pause and write notes in the margin, which is the signal of readers' meditation on the specific line and words. YA readers can practice meditation when they apply marginalia to their book reading.

Chapter 10

Finding Joy in *The Fault in Our Stars* through Florilegium

In the book *The Fault in Our Stars*, the main character, Hazel, meets Gus at a support group for teenagers with cancer. After the meeting she goes to Gus's house to watch a movie. When she enters the house, Hazel is struck by the multitude of pillows, framed needlepoint, and other objects that contain short messages. Gus explains that his parents call them "encouragements." One such message conveys that if there is no pain, we cannot know joy (p. 35). This is one of the core themes in the young adult novel, *The Fault in Our Stars*.

Joy is also one of the key concepts we find in sacred texts, including the Jewish scriptures contained in the *Tenakh*, the Christian New Testament, the *Quran*, the *Bhagavad Gita,* and other books. From a religious perspective, joy is a lifelong goal of attaining peace of mind and contentment in this world (and everlasting bliss in the hereafter.)

Joy is often interwoven with sorrow and pain. In the Judeo-Christian scriptures, for example, we read of Ruth, the Moabite daughter-in-law of the Jewish widow Naomi. Both women were in desperate circumstances for women in that society. Their husbands had died, leaving them destitute, without a man or family to take care of them. Naomi decided to return to the land of Judah and told Ruth to go back to her family, where Ruth would be able to remarry and be taken care of. Ruth chose to journey with Naomi and her God rather than go back to the religion of the culture she was raised in. She found joy in her friendship with Naomi and in her new adopted community.

Another example, from the Christian New Testament, is Paul, a Pharisee who hated and hunted Christians yet was touched by Jesus and transformed into one of the Jesus's greatest followers. He started many early churches and wrote several books of the New Testament. Imprisoned, threatened, and despised, his life was certainly not filled with material wealth and relaxation, yet while in prison he wrote the epistle to the Philippians, often called "The Book of Joy."

One explanation for how people can feel joy in difficult circumstances is that their faith allows them to see past the mundane to something that stretches beyond their earthly experience. Nobody can be happy while suffering emotional pain, excessive stress, or deep sorrow. But while happiness is a response to an immediate short-term situation, joy is tied to a person's connection to something beyond themselves. Joy can exist regardless of context or circumstances because that metaphysical connection makes them aware that they are not alone in those circumstances.

Instead, they feel connected to something greater and feel valued and sustained. Joy, in holy scriptures, is a way of life connected to hope and is not restricted to a person's current experience. Joy in young adult literature might focus on a character whose interest, value, concern, and love can help another character see past the pain and sorrow of life.

The Fault in Our Stars is about two teenagers who are dying of cancer—certainly not a novel where we would expect to find joy. In it, John Green explores joy in this moment in the lives of Hazel and Gus in the book, and students can discuss this theme through the practice of florilegium.

The Fault in Our Stars by Printz-award-winning author and social media influencer John Green debuted at number one on the New York Times Bestseller List and held that spot for seven consecutive weeks. John Green's other young adult novels include *Looking for Alaska* (2005), *Paper Towns* (2008), *An Abundance of Katherines* (2006) and *Turtles All The Way Down* (2017).

HAZEL AND GUS: FINDING JOY IN PAIN AND SORROW

The novel is told from the point of view of Hazel Grace Lancaster who was diagnosed with Stage IV thyroid cancer that spread to her lungs when she was 13. Since then, she has suffered from multiple types of mental and physical pain both from the cancer—including pneumonia, excessive swelling in the hands and feet, cracked skin, and coldness and blue lips due to lack of oxygen—and also from medical treatments—including radical neck dissection, radiation, and chemotherapy.

She meets Gus in a cancer support group that Hazel's mother encouraged her to attend. Gus's leg was amputated because of cancer. He is attending the group to support his friend Isaac, whose cancer is destroying his eyesight. The relationship nourishes both Hazel and Gus and enables them to be joyful while they battle cancer. It is necessary to know Hazel's pain before talking about her joy.

Healthy people breathe in and out constantly without thinking about it. To Hazel, however, her normal breathing depends on her oxygen tank, and a moment of separation from the tank threatens her life. Early in the book, when Hazel is reading outside, a little girl named Jackie asks about the cannula that supplies Hazel oxygen through her nostrils. When Hazel lets Jackie try it for a little bit, Hazel feels the difference immediately. She has to concentrate on her breathing until she gets the tubes back (p. 30).

Later in the book, Hazel has to take off the oxygen tank to go through security at the airport. Walking unencumbered and gaining back her sovereignty over her body amazes her, but her lungs feel like they are folding in upon themselves like flowers at dusk (p. 79). Hazel carries her disease with her everywhere she goes, the oxygen tank not only reminding her that she is sick but also drawing people's attention to her. She pulls the tank behind her the same way she pulls her pain with her everywhere she goes.

In addition to the constant dull pain in her daily life, Hazel sometimes has sharp pains that come out of nowhere. At one point in the story, Hazel has an incredibly painful headache caused by the fluid in her lungs and she must scream out to wake up her parents. On the way to the emergency room (ER), Hazel wishes she could die rather than suffer this pain. She ends up being hospitalized with that pain for six days. Hazel also experiences emotional pain from the doctor's evaluation of her health. Hazel's doctor does not view her as a strong candidate for a lung transplant, which indicates how hopeless her case is.

Another example of Hazel's emotional pain is the way she has to deal with the uncertainty of her life. Hazel has always wanted to meet the author of her favorite book, *An Imperial Affliction*, who lives in the Netherlands. Her cancer makes it difficult for her to even imagine planning such a trip. Her medical requirements and the uncertainty of her health from day to day mean that a trip to Europe seems unreachable. When she gets the chance to visit Amsterdam thanks to Gus's help and through the Make-a-Wish Foundation, she fears her health may decline, making the trip impossible.

Cancer not only causes Hazel physical pain but also stresses her mentally. The pain wells up when she thinks how her parents will be devastated by the loss of their only daughter. Hazel wishes that she never heard her mom saying that she didn't want to be a mom anymore during a trip to the intensive care unit (ICU) (p. 116). Her death will mean that her mother will never be able to think about Hazel and their experiences together without being immediately jarred by the fact that she is dead.

Gus quotes a line about how pain demands to be experienced from *An Imperial Affliction* in response to seeing his friend Isaac hurting (p. 57).

Isaac's girlfriend breaks up with him when she finds out he is going blind. Isaac cries while playing a video game with Gus and afterwards Gus encourages him to smash Gus's basketball trophies to vent. Isaac has lost the happiness he had found in his relationship with his girlfriend.

In contrast, for Hazel and Gus, joy appears in the midst of pain and suffering. Hazel's relationship with friends and parents has always been the source of her joy, but that joy grows as she falls in love with Gus. Hazel and Gus like each other's physical appearance, mind, and something else that is hard to define. Perhaps because of the way they both are facing death, this is not typical teenage puppy love, but a relationship characterized by deep levels of commitment, including a willingness to sacrifice for each other.

Like other couples, they often hang out together, read each other's favorite books, watch TV, and play video games, but Gus is willing to use his Make-a-Wish Foundation wish so that Hazel can realize her dream of meeting her favorite author. This represents a level of selflessness that is unusual in high school relationships. That trip becomes the highlight of both of their young lives, and the joy they feel is as real as their pain. The limited days of their courtship may not be filled with constant dancing and singing, but they are filled with laughter, understanding, love, and courage in the face of death—a kind of deep joy.

While Hazel bemoans having to drag her body, ruined by cancer, around for years, she decides that her relationship with Gus makes it worth the difficulty, the breathing equipment and tubes and the constant treachery of the tumors (p. 109). At the end of the book she speaks directly to Gus about how filled with gratitude she is for what seems like an infinity of time they had together. She thinks of it as an eternity within days that are numbered (p. 142). When we compare these two ideas, we can see Hazel's progression from seeing her body as a heavy weight that keeps her from joy, to discovering that Gus loves her body even in its brokenness, to Gus's love for her and her broken body making her feel like she can touch the infinite.

At the end of that progression, Hazel views her life through an entirely new lens—joy. Even as a patient of a terminal disease, even of deep uncertainties regarding how long she and Gus will be alive, Hazel's love for Gus brings her more joy than other relationships and transforms the way she sees her life.

Hazel's joy is the presence and company of Gus, who she loves so much, who reads her mind, appreciates her beauty, cares for her, and supports her in times of despair. She describes how she likes the sound of his voice, his stories, his name, and his smile. Gus invites Hazel to join him in going through the lows and highs together and in supporting Isaac together. Even when Hazel demurs, refusing to kiss him, fearing that a romantic relationship will lead only to pain, he accepts these new terms of their relationship without hesitation. Gus values, appreciates, and affirms Hazel, which boosts her confidence and hope.

In his book *Movies are Prayers*, Larsen references the Apu trilogy of movies by Indian writer/director Satyajit Ray. It depicts a Hindu couple who, after heaviness in their past and before sorrow in their future, find joy in being with each other. After a summary of the film, Larsen concludes, "It recalls the Christian concept of joy in the midst of suffering, of emphasizing celebration even in a sorrowful world" (2017, p. 163). Larsen could have written that sentence in response to *The Fault in Our Stars*.

Likewise, Gus's 17-year life is replete with suffering and joy. He loses his leg in his first bout of cancer. When cancer reoccurs, he loses control of his bladder when sleeping, and cannot even pick anything up by himself. Nevertheless, in his last days, Gus squeezes Hazel's hand, reminding her that it is a good life that they are living (p. 128). Evidently, Hazel's love enables him to be joyful and grateful for his short life.

Gus's relationship with Hazel is a highlight in his life, and his life quality is good for him despite the pain of cancer. He goes through the last phase of his life with a girl he loves from the bottom of his heart, still experiences life with her, helps her realize one of her dreams, and cheers her up. His self-awareness and nearly transcendent love for Hazel allows him, a person whose life would certainly justify bitterness and anger, to exclaim at several points in the book that it is a good life.

HAZEL'S PARENTS: TAKING JOY WHILE THEY CAN

Hazel's parents model a joyous life as they grapple with their only daughter's terminal cancer. They enjoy being parents while also feeling the sorrow and despair associated with Hazel's ailment. The novel features Hazel's mom more than her dad, so this section will as well.

When Hazel is rushed to the ER and hospitalized in the ICU, her mom fears that she might soon no longer be a mom (p. 116). It is heart-wrenching for parents to lose their only child, and even the fear of losing a child is hard. When Hazel compares herself to a grenade, her mom responds that the joy Hazel brings into their lives is much more powerful than the sadness they feel about her cancer (p. 60). Hazel's parents believe they can live with her cancer. They value Hazel's life, presence, and company more than her illness; the former is priceless, and the latter can never strip them of the memories they have spent together. The words they use reveal their joy and gratitude in stormy life.

The joy of Hazel's mom is also revealed in the way she finds any excuse to celebrate life with Hazel: Hazel's half birthday, or holidays that are less frequently celebrated in the US, including Bastille Day. Celebration of even a distressing life conveys the attitude of joy.

Hazel's mom, by Hazel's standards, is her best friend, and Gus is the second one behind her. The relationship with her daughter brings her mom joy in spite of her daughter's battle with cancer. In addition, she is thankful for each day she has with her daughter and takes joy in the little moments that she has, since she will likely never see her daughter graduate from college, get married, have children, or many other big days in life.

ISAAC: CONFRONTING LIFE WITH COURAGE AND JOY

Isaac, like Hazel and Gus, is a teenager and cancer patient. He loses his eyesight because of cancer, which subsequently causes his girlfriend to break up with him. Cancer is overwhelming for a young adult, but Isaac's friendship with Gus and Hazel sustains him through a tough time. Isaac is never alone. Rather, Gus and Hazel journey with him, listen to him, and let him vent his despair and disappointment, in hopes that he will be able to find joy, or at least happiness. It is up for interpretation whether Isaac finds anything like joy—perhaps the closest he comes is humor derived from a grim sarcasm.

After Isaac's eye surgery, Gus and Hazel tease Isaac about his own situation. Isaac's sense of humor is undampened when Hazel visits him after he undergoes his surgery. Even through the most intense pain he jokes that Hazel should come closer so that he can touch her face and see deeper into her inner identity than someone who wasn't blind ever could (p. 45). The courage to confront the new and dark phase of life with laughter means that his inside world is bright, although the outside is dark. In his eulogy to Gus, Isaac says that he does not want to be able to see in a world where there is no Gus (p. 141), which shows his friend enlightens his world so that he can laugh under the most miserable circumstances.

PETER VAN HOUTEN: THE LOSS OF JOY

Peter Van Houten, the author of Hazel's favorite book, *An Imperial Affliction*, serves as a foil for Hazel and Gus. When Hazel and Gus visit him in Amsterdam they do not find the smart and funny and understanding writer they expect. Instead they find a man who has not experienced joy since his young daughter died of cancer.

Van Houten turns out to be a wretched man who seems to be alive only so that he can lash out at other people and make them hurt like he does (p.

151). He is the only character in the novel with no supportive relationship. He refuses to connect with anyone. He alienates his assistant and retreats into despair and alcohol whenever possible. When Hazel and Gus come to visit Van Houten, at the invitation of his assistant, he behaves horribly. Hazel walks out, and Gus confronts Van Houten and challenges him to treat people with civility. Peter later attends Gus's funeral and shows care and concern for Hazel, and remorse for his behavior. This may be the beginning of his search for joy (though it is unclear if he will ever find it).

FLORILEGIUM

McKillop (2020) summarizes florilegium, dating it back to ancient Greek times and continuing to develop through the classical period and taking hold with Christian authors in the third century. A florilegium was originally a collection of quotes or excerpts from important texts or scriptures. The first florilegia were collections of the sayings of Jesus or the apostles.

Florilegia, as used by Zoltan and ter Kuile in the "Harry Potter and the Sacred Text" podcast, is a practice of reading and pondering, of conversing with literature by pulling out the phrases that "sparkle," removing them from their original context and considering them in the context of the entire life and the reader's experiences. Fresh meanings may be discovered in this aggregation of sparklets and in their conversation with each other. Seeing quotes in new contexts may generate new ideas, create questions, illuminate beauty, or call up conundrums.

There are two ways for students to practice florilegium in class. We have found that it is best to demonstrate florilegium with the entire class the first time you use it. In this case, the teacher asks everyone in the class to find a sentence in a particular chapter that somehow connects them to the theme of joy.

Once everyone has selected a sentence, the teacher chooses students to read their sentence and tell why that quote took their attention. Why did they pick it? Why do they love it? The teacher then puts the quote up on the board. We have found that it is effective to have students vote on their favorite two quotes. Another option is for the teacher to choose two quotes that connect to a particular theme the class is exploring with the book.

The teacher then asks a student to read the two quotes together, back to back, as if there were no gap between them. Then the teacher asks if anyone is struck by the way those two quotes interact. (If necessary, the teacher can share her or his insights about the two quotes, but it would be better to have a few students respond first.) It is important to emphasize, when calling on students, that any insight will be welcomed and appreciated.

Then the teacher asks another student to read the quotes back to back again, but this time with their order reversed. Again the teacher calls upon students and/or asks the general group for insights about the two quotes working together. These responses can be both connected to the theme and also about anything at all.

Once students are familiar with how florilegium works, they can work with partners, each one picking a sentence that strikes them on the theme of joy in the book. Each student explains the context of the sentence, then one reads both sentences and the partners discuss what they think about connections between the two sentences. Afterwards, they read the two sentences again with the order reversed and again discuss the connection between the two sentences.

For example, let us suppose we have done this exercise with the class and they have chosen two sentences pertaining to the theme of joy that we mentioned earlier. First a sentence about how all of the pain and suffering that comes with dragging around a body broken by cancer, dependent on medical equipment, oxygen tanks and ports and IVs, and all the setbacks and false hopes, is made worth it for Hazel through her love for Gus which he returns (p. 109).

The second sentence is much shorter, simply a reminder from Gus to Hazel that their life is good (p. 128).

The student who suggests the first sentence explains that it is what Hazel thought after Gus kissed her for publicly for the first time in a museum in Amsterdam. The student chose that quote because of how it shows a major change in the way Hazel views her body—a movement from seeing her body as something that is always dragging her down and getting in her way, to viewing her body as a good thing. The student also makes a connection to her own life and how running track taught her to appreciate her body rather than hate it. She thinks it speaks to the theme of joy because Hazel's change in attitude is a movement from despising her body toward taking joy in it.

The student who suggests the second sentence explains that Gus says this when he and Hazel are hanging out in his backyard after his cancer has recurred and he knows these are his last days. The student says they chose this sentence because Gus's thinking is shifting too. Earlier in the book, the student says, Gus seemed funny, but also cynical. He and Hazel made fun of the support group and of people who would give them cancer perks. This quote however, shows that Gus has concluded that in spite of all the pain and limitations, life can still be good, and even joyful, mostly because of his relationship with Hazel.

The student cannot think of a connection to his own life. The teacher then reads the two sentences again, but back to back, as if they follow each other in the text. The class discusses this pairing of texts, and a student points out that one subtheme she noticed is how all through the book, joy and pain are not exclusive and that pain doesn't preclude joy. Another student suggests that, in the book, sorrow almost functions as soil in which joy can grow. A third student points to the sentence she had suggested (but which was not chosen) which fits well here—it is a quote from one of the Encouragements scattered in frames and pillows in Gus's home about how pain makes joy possible. The discussion continues connecting to other parts of the book and students' own experiences.

When the discussion begins to lose energy, the teacher rereads the sentences, this time inverting the order. The teacher reads slowly and thoughtfully, giving the students time to reflect on the ways that the sentences inform each other.

The teacher calls on a student who has not contributed yet and asks if that student has any insights. That student says that, on hearing the new arrangement of sentence, he thought about how nobody's life is completely painless in the world, so how to be joyful in a sorrowful life is a question everyone faces. This leads to some examples from the students' lives of times when people they know have dealt with difficult situations. The teacher lets several students weigh in, then directs the discussion back to what the two sentences have to say to each other.

One student points out that in this arrangement, it almost seems like Hazel is talking to herself, starting off with the conclusion that in spite of everything, it is a good life—then thinking about how her body, which she has always thought of as a burden to carry, has actually carried her through some interesting places and amazing experiences.

The discussion continues from there.

It is important to recognize that the exercise is not dependent upon picking two sentences that fit perfectly with each other. There are easily fifty and maybe more like a hundred different sentences in *The Fault in Our Stars* that can lead to equally fruitful discussions. It is not as if there are two magical sentences that your students must hunt down that will open the interpretive key to the whole book.

Rather, the magic comes when we focus on almost any small part of a well-written book. In that moment, a sentence or two becomes a door that leads to our consideration of the larger story. Florilegium help students stay deeply focused on the text while making connections to their own lives without wandering into shallower territory and away from the theme the class is considering. The selected sentences bring students back to the text again and again.

HELPING STUDENTS UNDERSTAND JOY

Why do we bother with teaching literature to our students? One common answer is that novels, poems, plays, and other literature help students understand what it means to be human. If we are serious about that, we need to make sure that the material we teach and the way that we teach that material really does help them understand themselves.

Hazel and Gus in *The Fault in Our Stars* exemplify for us a life of joy and suffering. They never deny the physical and mental pain they go through, but they are joyful because of the relationships they have built with each other, family, and friends. How real is their pain? How real is their joy? They give people struggling with pain hope, and inspire them in their circumstance to discover joy. It is safe to say that John Green is writing a prayer of joy by focusing on people whom we would expect would be the least joyful people in the world.

Chapter 11

The Inquisitor's Tale
Using PaRDeS to Explore Pilgrimage

Making a pilgrimage is a major part of many religious traditions. While in the modern world, Muslims can often drive or fly to Mecca, and Jewish people and Christians can go to the holy land of Jerusalem, in the ancient world a pilgrimage often involved arduous travel and difficult conditions. The idea of a pilgrimage is that the journey itself is a form of asceticism, of self-discipline and denial, which brings about personal and spiritual growth in the pilgrim.

What we variously call quest novels, heroes' journeys, or road trip stories in literature, are all founded upon the idea of pilgrimage—that when characters move geographically, in seeking something physical, those characters are also moving themselves to a new emotional or spiritual perspective, that they are seeking answers to questions, and that completing that journey does not merely involve arriving at a place, finishing a journey, or fulfilling a quest for something tangible, but that it involves discovering, realizing, internalizing, or reaching an epiphany.

Adam Gidwitz's *The Inquisitor's Tale: or the Three Children and Their Holy Dog*, won both a Newbery Honor and the Sydney Taylor Book Award in 2017 and was a *New York Times* bestseller. Drawing from six years of historical research into the world of medieval France, Gidwitz borrows the form of Chaucer's *Canterbury Tales,* in which travelers at an inn each contribute part of the story.

In *The Inquisitor's Tale*, however, the listener to these tales is actually an inquisitor sent by the Church to determine if the children are heretics. The children in question—a peasant girl named Jeanne who can see the future, a half-Saracen boy named William who was raised by monks and is capable of feats of astounding strength, and a young Jewish boy named Jacob gifted with an extraordinary ability to heal, joined by a dog who died saving Jeanne from a snake and is now miraculously returned—eventually set out on a quest to save hundreds of Jewish holy books from being burned by the Christian king of France.

The Inquisitor's Tale may push the boundaries of what counts as a YA book because the main characters in the book seem younger than we typically think the characters in a YA book should be. Yet the complexity of the book and the themes it addresses make us think that the book is more appropriate for high school students than younger readers.

This book also offers opportunities to not only to talk with students about valuing different religious traditions, and understanding how people lived and thought differently during the medieval period, but it is also an amazing example of using the techniques we have discussed earlier in this book to help them explore a pilgrimage narrative and what each character discovers.

EXPLORING THE THEME OF PILGRIMAGE IN *THE INQUISITOR'S TALE*

Throughout this book we have been emphasizing two ideas. First, that we can see YA novels collectively as prayers, interactions between the readers, the writer, and a theme that gets at larger, perhaps universal ideas of how humans connect to each other, what our purpose is, or what our place is in the universe. The other idea is that instead of discussing these themes abstractly or in summary, we can use tools originally developed by looking at sacred texts to consider smaller scenes, paragraphs, or even lines, and that doing so will provide us with a grounded entry point to a more fruitful discussion.

This second idea assumes that in the strongest YA books, those themes run so strong and so deep that they are easy to connect to from almost any line. *The Inquisitor's Tale* is an excellent example of just such a book. Instead of providing a full orderly analysis of the ways in which the book functions as a prayer of pilgrimage, we will look at how that potential would come out in a class using PaRDeS as a discussion method.

POTENTIAL FOR PaRDeS

We have written throughout this book about how looking at small passages—a paragraph, a couple of sentences, a phrase or even a word—can link us to other expressions of that theme, other connections, other understandings. The sacred text reading process of PaRDeS is described by Vanessa Zoltan in her book *Praying with Jane Eyre* (and also in Chapter 3). She lists four steps to the process. After the reader selects a sentence that they love:

Step 1: (*p'shat*/surface reading) Ask yourself, "What is the intended meaning of the sentence? What did the author want me to get from it?"
Step 2: (*remez*/hints): Pick one word from the sentence and trace it throughout the book. Think about all the different ways the word is used in the book.
Step 3: (*d'rash*/seek): Ask yourself, "What is the lesson that I want to pull from this sentence?"
Step 4 (*sud*/secret): After you have done all this work, you have traced a word and figured out what lesson you might draw from it, now the text will open up one of its secrets to you. (Zoltan, 2021, pp. 236–40)

In the same book, Zoltan also provides suggestions for determining the best books to engage discussion. She suggests that, for a good book to result in a good discussion, it has to be really complicated (p. 11). What she means by this is not that the book needs to be incomprehensible, but that it be layered and connected—in short, that there be a lot to be uncovered, unraveled, and discovered. This does not mean that the book needs to have hidden meanings.

English Language Arts teachers are familiar with the refrain from some students that English class involves teachers revealing the hidden meanings of books, as if the author would deliberately hide the point of what they are writing. Such thinking comes from teachers telling students an interpretation and requiring them to memorize it instead of providing structures for the students to uncover the meaning on their own. In truth, discussion can help students peel the layers themselves and discover meanings that are not hidden, but deeper.

The Inquisitor's Tale is a remarkably rich text, and we would suggest that it is author Adam Gidwitz's prayer of pilgrimage. The idea of pilgrimage is a major part of the journey of at least five of the characters in the story, and each character's interaction with the idea of pilgrimage is very different from the others.

PaRDeS offers the opportunity for students to trace that theme in the story and see how everything connects and extends the ideas running through *The Inquisitor's Tale*. Most of the previous chapters of this book have begun with a summary of the book and its themes, and have ended with a description of how the sacred reading practice would look in the classroom. In this chapter, we will stitch together several classroom experiences to show both how students can interact with the text, but also the depth of potential for discovery.

SELECTING A QUOTE FOR PaRDeS

When Bill starts off working with PaRDeS in the classroom, he asks students to nominate passages that would work as the focus of the exercise. In the case of *The Inquisitor's Tale*, Bill's students came up with five nominations. They are:

1. From page 191, a quote predicting that there will be a book burning, a huge number of books on the fire.
2. From page 263, a quote that observes that if God can save the souls of Christians, he can, of course, save Jacob's soul as well.
3. From page 336, a quote in which Michelangelo tells the children that it is their job to continue to bear witness against foolishness and meanness.
4. From page 115, a short quote about wanting to know.
5. From page 300 another short quote acknowledging that the church was wrong.

Sometimes Bill lets his students vote on which passage to focus on. Sometimes he picks at random. In this case, however, based on multiple readings of the book, he selects the second passage about God saving Jacob because he knows it is a pivotal passage—one that stands at a junction between several key moments in the narrative.

For this particular example, we will assume that the students have read the whole book and the class is going to discuss the entire book in a single class session. Of course, teachers could also choose to do this exercise after a single chapter or break the book into quarters or halves and have a discussion of each section of the book.

STEP 1: P'SHAT/SURFACE MEANING

This passage appears in the midst of one of the most important scenes of the book. The children who are the main characters—Jeanne (a peasant who has seizures in which she can see the future), William (A young Christian monk born of a Saracen woman of Northern Africa and a Christian knight who fought in the crusades—and who is capable of great strength) and Jacob (a young Jewish boy who lost his parents in a fire set by Christian ruffians and has demonstrated miraculous healing abilities)—have teamed up with a giant monk named Michelangelo and are hoping to prevent the King of France from burning thousands of Jewish holy books.

Students might describe the literal meaning of the passage in different ways, though, depending on which character's eyes they see this scene through. Jeanne for example, has just confessed to Michelangelo that she wants to rescue the books from being burned, but she isn't sure she wants to sacrifice her life to do so. She asks him if, regardless of the amount of wisdom contained in a book, is it morally right to die for it (p. 255)?

And here is the question that Jeanne has been thinking about, but has avoided asking for most of their pilgrimage. What is life worth? How should you spend it? What responsibility does one have for how one spends one's own life?

Eventually the preparations are complete and the King's cryer announces that if any Jewish person converts to Christianity, the King will pay him forty gold coins. In reaction to this, the narrator relates that when they first met, William and Jeanne might have pleaded with Jacob to renounce his Jewish upbringing, followed Christ, and, in that way, avoid being condemned to hell. Now that they know each other, however, the idea of asking Jacob to renounce who he is seems ridiculous. And this is the moment in the scene when we hear the sentence the class is focusing on. The children have discovered that, apart from what they call their religions and what languages they pray in, there seem to be few differences between them. And all of them thought the idea of being paid to convert was even more laughable. What kind of a person of faith would put their beliefs up for sale (p. 263)?

In this moment we see not only the spiritual journey that Jeanne has been on, but the journey they have all made in their understanding of God and themselves and the society they live in. Jacob's journey is simultaneously deepening his own faith and being accepting and welcoming of the ways that others worship. And Jacob's presence has had an impact on the attitudes (and pilgrimages) of the others as well.

William had begun the story frightened of spending time with peasants and Jewish people, for he had been told they were evil and would lead him, as a devout monk, astray. At this point in the book, however, William affirms that what matters is not so much the differences in theology or politics, or religious observance—but what matters is the friendship that has grown between these children, and their dedication to saving some of the books consigned to the flames as a result of unreasoning hate. He has come to a point where who he is and what he believes is becoming clear to him.

Gidwitz is emphasizing the idea that it is easy to think a certain way about someone when you generalize them into a box—but when we know people as themselves, it is harder to hold on to stereotypes and divisions.

STEP 2: REMEZ/HINTS

Remez is the next step in the practice, in which we pick one word and trace its other occurrences through the book. In the case of the chosen passage, Bill suggests his students focus on the word *follow*, as it ties in most directly with the theme of pilgrimage.

In the classroom, one approach might be to divide the book between several small groups of students and assign each of them a section of the book. Sometimes, though, it works better to ask them more generally if they can think of a moment when there is something involving the concept of following that occurs in the story.

One student recalls how following is part of the story almost from the start. Because Jeanne's parents had to work in the fields all day, when she was little, they had to leave her in their hovel, guarded by their faithful greyhound, Gwenforte. When a poisonous adder creeps in, Gwenforte moves little Jeanne to a safe corner of the room, then kills the snake, spraying blood across the room. When Jeanne's parents return from work, they don't see that their daughter, only the dog, covered with blood. Jumping to conclusions, they kill the dog, then find Jeanne safe and sound. Filled with remorse, they bury the dog in a beautiful grove in the forest.

That grove becomes a place where villagers bring newborn babies, that they might be blessed by Gwenforte's protection. Jeanne grows older and begins to have visions of the future. She sees a vision of men with torches and axes coming to burn down the grove and a white greyhound standing against them. Soon that vision comes to pass. The men have been sent to stamp out what they consider to be a heretic shrine, because peasants are following a holy dog instead of following church-approved saints. As a result of this concern, Jeanne is taken prisoner and hauled off to Saint-Denis to be tried for heresy.

Another student says that passage has more than just the villagers following the holy ghost dog. She says this moment is the beginning of Jeanne's pilgrimage, even though Jeanne is not clear what she is following. She is not trying to learn or discover or find something. She is not seeking anything but the return to her parents. She has no control of where she is going or what might happen. She isn't on a quest for faith, or to rid herself of doubt, or to find God.

She is following a path without reason and without knowing where it will lead. And she doesn't understand why the soldiers, who are supposed to serving God (and their feudal lord), choose to follow a path of hatred and anger.

Another student suggests that the children, later in the story, follow Michelangelo di Bologna. Bill asks the student to explain further and the student elaborates. Early in the book, the children are on a journey to speak with Hubert the Good. They believe he will be offer them advice and protection. But they are surprised to find that Hubert is anything but good. He threatens to kill Gwenforte and after that the children as well. It is Michelangelo di Bologna who saves them and when Gwenforte trots after Michelangelo, the children follow. When they are safely away, Michelangelo explains that he believes they are saints. Then he introduces the subject of their quest.

He tells them that he is trying to accomplish something important and he needs their special talents to pull it off. He explains that there will be a book burning, a great bonfire. He tells the group that the books will be piled up like logs in the middle of Paris and they will be lit on fire (p. 191). The books in danger are Jewish holy books that the French king believes must be destroyed.

Michelangelo then gives them two options. They could join him in trying to prevent the books form being burned—but if they do that they will face those that hate them; they will face persecution; and they may even face martyrdom. They would, however, be fighting for what is right, for that which is good, and for the wisdom contained in the books.

Or, the other option is they could return to what is left of their lives.

The student says that Michelangelo is asking the children to follow him. Jeanne is the one who responds for all three children. She sits up straight and says that they will walk boldly. She says they will be saints (p. 191). The student points out that the children's choice to follow Michelangelo is motivated not by who the church considers to be good, nor by what society considers to be the right thing (as clearly the majority of society follows King Louis, who is the one who has called for the books to be burned.) Instead, they are following Michelangelo because rescuing the books seems like the right thing to do.

A third student recalls that when we are introduced to William, it is a scene where he chooses not to follow one of his teachers. When we first meet William, he is an extremely talkative and inquisitive member of a community of silence. Brother Bartholomew, one of William's teachers, lectures the boys in the monastery school about how peasants and Jews are all tools of the Devil. William questions what his teacher is saying. How could all Jews be evil? Wouldn't that include Moses and Abraham, and King David from the Bible? He thinks of Jewish books he has read, by Rashi and Rabbi Yahuda, which seem full of wisdom to him.

Brother Bartholomew goes on to say that all women are also in league with the Devil. William questions this as well. He wonders if what Brother Bartholomew says can possibly apply to every woman. After all, he reasons, everyone was born from a woman. He also thinks of Hildegard of Bingen whose amazing writings William has read. And the Virgin Mary was a woman as well, as was Mary Magdalene. Finally he thinks of all the female saints there have been (p. 37).

But again, before William can finish reasoning it out, Bartholomew has moved on. He begins railing against the Saracens. William has never liked the word *Saracen* as it imprecisely refers to both a Muslim and a foreigner in general. William is also not sure if he is a Saracen. He has been raised as a Christian and has devoted his life to Christian service—but does his dark skin and hair mean that he is a Saracen? Bartholomew continues with his screed, arguing that peasants are the slaves of the Devil, that Jews are the emissaries of the Devil, that women are the spies of the Devil, and that Saracens act as the Devil's infantrymen (p. 38).

As a result of this lecture, William chooses not to follow Brother Bartholomew, but instead challenges him. What about Muslim scholars who preserved the words of Aristotle, he asks. What about Muslim mathematicians who invented the concept of the Zero? Bartholomew is unmoved. William brings up the time when another monk consulted the writings of a Muslim physician and saved Brother Bartholomew's life.

Bartholomew, now backed into a corner, loses whatever control he had and accuses William of defending the Devil's allies. He then calls William a brown bastard and concedes that at least William is not a Saracen whore like his mother was (p. 39).

And so William first appears to the reader as a very bright scholar who is brave enough to choose not to follow his teacher when he knows that teacher is wrong. But William's questions in this section are just that, questions. He knows that Brother Bartholomew cannot be completely right, but he isn't sure that Brother Bartholomew is completely wrong either. Later in the book, we see that William still struggles with these ideas. He might not think that Jews are agents of the Devil, but he distrusts and dislikes Jewish people (and peasants, and women). Part of William's quest is learning whether to follow Brother Bartholomew's teachings or his own experience.

As a result of William's decision not to follow along with Brother Bartholomew's invective, William is expelled from the school and the monastery in which he has lived his whole life. Thus William's spiritual pilgrimage begins not with his own choice to seek something out, but, like Jeanne, with being thrown out into the world. And so begins William's search for understanding about how he should respond to those people who he has been told are evil—Jewish people, peasants, and women.

At this point three students have brought up scenes in which the idea of following plays an important part. A teacher might be tempted to stop asking for more on the theory for which soon the discussion will run out. But Bill, knowing he is pushing his students, asks if anyone else has a connection to another part in the story that connects to the word *follow*?

A fourth student responds. In chapter 7, the student says, William meets a group of actual pilgrims. William approaches them with good cheer in hopes of being able to follow them and join their quest. A man and his son, however, demand that William remove his mask. William, dumbfounded, then explains that he is not wearing a mask. At this point the man draws a hatchet and says, that whether William is a highway robber or a demon, he should leave them (p. 70). William explains that he is not a brigand or a devil, but a Benedictine monk, devoted to God. He is lonely and is wondering if he can walk with them a while. The son, with wild eyes, repeats his father's word, "Begone!"

And with that, William, in the midst of his own pilgrimage, is turned away by another group of pilgrims, shunned by people who presumably are on a pilgrimage based on their own Christian faith. He is told not to follow them in their quest to follow God. Their common beliefs, which should act as something to bind them together, do not seem to connect them at all.

And then later, down the road, William comes upon the same group. The wheel has fallen off their cart. With his great strength (and in a scene reminiscent of Jean Valjean lifting the cart off the injured man in *Les Misérables*) William picks up the cart and encourages the pilgrims to put the wheel back on, while he holds it. They stare, open-mouthed. He explains again that he is a Christian monk. They do not respond. Finally, he drops the cart and, shrugging, says that he tried and is on his way (p. 72).

When Bill asks why this scene took the student's attention, the student responds that they doubt that such an experience would actually be easy for William to shrug off. The pilgrims called him a demon, based only on his dark skin. The student wonders if William might make the connection between this experience and Brother Bartholomew declaring that all Jews are agents of the Devil. Bill points out that, if William makes that connection, the author does not tell us so—and goes on to say that such moments, left up to the reader, make the reading experience a deeply personal one.

Another student raises a hand and wants to talk about another case of following. At the end of the book the children, carrying the books, must cross the causeway to Mont-Saint-Michel. The causeway is dangerous, even in low tide, and so the children must follow the old innkeeper and step exactly where he steps. When they are halfway across, the king's army comes thundering down the slope after them. They ride their horses out into the tidal flats, and then the importance of following becomes clear as the knights and horses begin disappearing into the quicksand. In this scene, following closely is literally a matter of life and death, says the student.

Another student points out that it is during this scene that the children rescue Blanche, the mother of the king, who has been unkind to them. Bill agrees, but asks what that has to do with following. The student explains that although the children are supposed to follow the king and the queen mother they choose not to in favor of following what they know to be right—the rescuing of the books.

Bill wraps things up at this point, writing on the board some of the ideas the discussion has brought up and which students might want to continue talking out in later class sessions or in written assignments.

STEP 3: D'RASH/SEEK

Bill transitions to step 3 in PaRDeS: *D'rash* or seeking. He suggests the students should ask themselves what lessons they want to pull from the passage. He also explains that the idea here isn't that the book has a single moral or practical message, but that the ideas the students have in response to what they read may have, upon reflection, some bearing on all of their lives.

Bill rereads the passage, then reminds students that the larger theme they are looking at is one of pilgrimage. After giving the students some time to reflect, he asks again, "What does this book have to say to you? How does it connect to your life? Is there a passage that you think leads you to understanding?"

A student raises his hand. He mentions a scene near the beginning of the book when the knights (who are taking Jeanne to Saint-Denis to stand trial for being a heretic) stop at an inn. They catch a young boy who they decide is a thief. When they are about to kill him, Jeanne, with a rope around her own neck like a leash, calls out in a strong commanding voice for them to stop and to leave the boy alone! This brave moment leads to the rescue of Jacob by William and to all three of the children slipping away from the inn.

The student explains that he admires Jeanne for being so brave in this moment and speaking out against something that was wrong, even when she had very little power and a lot to risk. He also says that he isn't sure the scene is very realistic because Jeanne's speaking up, combined with William's appearance, somehow resulted in them escaping. The student isn't sure that speaking up always works out that well.

Another student jumps in. She says she just realized something—that just after that scene you would think their pilgrimage would really begin. But, in fact, the three children are escaping from something, not journeying toward something. After they escape, while hiding in the forest, they tell their stories to each other, but the only plan they have about where to go is anywhere that will allow them to escape Michelangelo di Bologna (who they believe is after them).

And another student chimes in that really they just want to stay with their friends. When William says they should go to Saint-Denis to plead their case to Abbot Hubert the Good, the others agree, but their journey is still motivated not so much by following, but by fleeing.

The first student wonders if a pilgrimage necessarily has to be a movement from one place to another. Couldn't it be like a mental voyage of discovery or whatever? The third student responds that Jeanne is not seeking answers to questions, she is seeking safety. And when she has a seizure and sees a dragon menacing them in the future, that is a vision of fear, not seeking

A student who has been quiet up until now asks if his comment has to be about pilgrimage.

Bill says that it does not.

"Well," says the student, "I have a favorite quote. It is from the time in the inn, when Jeanne is remembering that stinky cheese from the part before the dragon. That was the cheese that Jeanne said tasted like life. Then Jeanne asked something about how there can be so much pain and victory mixed together" (p. 279).

Bill asks the student if he can give a bit more context for the quote. The student says he can't remember, so Bill opens it up to others in the class. One of the students, who spoke before, raises her hand. "It is just before the scene with the drunken friar."

Bill asks her to elaborate.

The student flips through her book, then explains that the scene involves a drunken friar at the next table who overhears Jeanne and butts in because he hears someone discussing theology. She reads from the text and gives the class the drunken man's words. Essentially, he argues that the hardest question to answer in all of theology is how an all-powerful God can let bad things happen. The children agree that this is what they are wondering about. Then the man asks them who they are. They don't understand, but then he tells them about a moment in scripture, in the book of Job, and how Job questions the horrible things God let happen to him. God asks Job who he is. He asks if Job was there when God created the blue whale, If Job wasn't there then—in short, if Job isn't God, how can Job know what is just or unjust—what is right and wrong? In the same way, the drunken monk continues, how can the children know what God's plans are and what he is thinking (p. 281).

Another student jumps in to ask if she can respond to the discussion before about how pilgrimages can be more than just a geographical journey. This student says that Jacob is also going on an internal pilgrimage. Since Jacob is outside of his insular Jewish community for the first time, he is testing to find out if people who are not Jewish can be good and caring—particularly Jeanne, a Christian, and William, a Christian whose mother was Muslim. The student mentions a discussion between Jacob and William that highlights the differences and moments of unity between the children's different religious faiths.

When Jeanne asks who Rabbi Yehuda is, William answers that he is a famous heathen. Jacob asks if William means that Yehuda is a Jewish writer. William says yes. Jacob says Yehuda is very famous. William uses the word notorious. When Jacob says that Yehuda is wise, William argues that he is wicked. When Jacob says that Yehuda is learned, William yells that he is learned in the ways of the evil one. Jacob yells back that Yehuda's writing is beautiful and, surprisingly, William agrees, admitting that Yehuda writes with more beauty than any other author he knows.

Jacob responds that although William may be an idolater, he does have good taste (p. 158). The student argues that both boys discover that a member of a group they have always been taught to dismiss, disdain, or perhaps actually hate, is not so different as they thought.

Another student says that William seems to be seeking and finding out the same thing.

Though Bill suspects that there is more to be said about which characters are engaging in which pilgrimages and what that means in terms of following, he also recognizes that it might be best to end this part of the exercise while the students still have interest in the subject, and so he suggests it is time to move to the last step of PaRDeS.

STEP 4: SUD/SECRET

Bill reminds the students of the good work they have already done with *The Inquisitor's Tale*. He reminds them that they have traced a word and figured out what lesson they might draw from the text. He suggests that now they should open themselves up to the possibilities of what secrets the text might have to show them. He asks the students to write in their journals for five minutes to give them time to consider the question. After the journal writing is done, Bill opens the floor for the students to share any secrets they see in the text.

One student raises her hand and wants to talk about a particular scene. Just before they put their plan into action to save the books from burning, Jeanne takes William's hand in one of hers, and Jacob's hand in the other. Jacob whispers that he thinks they should pray. William asks if it should be a Christian prayer or a Jewish prayer. Jacob replies that he doubts that it even matters (p. 259).

The student then skips forward in the book to a scene after the children's rescue plan didn't work and they have lost their friend Michelangelo and after they remembered the books that were in the satchels that William brought on his donkey. The children discover that some of the books that the Christian King Louis wanted to burn were Bibles written in Hebrew. The book burners were going to burn their own holy book. And it is Jacob who, after the Inquisitor confesses his intentions toward them, and after the children forgive him, reads in the Talmud the line, "Whoever destroys a single life destroys the whole world. And whoever saves a life saves the whole world."

The student says that really what the students discovered was bigger than just the idea that people who come from different religions can get along—they find out that all religions believe that all of life is deeply sacred, and caring for each other and the work that humans do in their lives means saving the whole world. Bill thanks the student for the excellent insight. He asks if anyone else has a secret that the text is revealing to them.

A student who has not yet spoken in the discussion raises his hand. He wants to talk about something even later in the book than the previous comment. It is when the children have been reunited with Michelangelo. The Inquisitor narrator describes the moment saying that they all stand, amazed at the weighty monk petting Jeanne's white dog. The narrator points out that both the dog and Michelangelo are heavenly pilgrims (p. 332).

Then Jacob asks why God sent Gwenforte back from the dead. He asks why God gave them miracles to perform. He asks why God put them through so much difficulty. Michelangelo explains by listing all of the good they have done. But Jacob is still wondering why God doesn't just fix the world with a single poof. Michelangelo explains that God does not work that way, that he works through people. Like Jacob. Jacob ends the conversation by saying that God runs the world in some strange ways (p. 332–33).

The student says that he likes the way the book ends. That there are no answers, not really. That some stuff just stays a mystery, no matter how hard we try to figure it out.

Another student (speaking somewhat out of turn) doesn't understand why they would read the whole book just to find out that there is no point to it. Bill is about to offer a rejoinder, but the first student responds that the mystery is the point. He says that the characters in the book hint at some reasons why bad things and good things in life maybe make some sense but that in the end the fact that it remains a mystery is kind of cool. The interrupting student doesn't seem convinced.

Bill comments that he thinks this is something they might want to think about for a while. He then asks if anybody else has any secrets from the text.

Another student raises a hand. They say they aren't quite sure what the secret is, but they want to talk about the scene after the children have met Michelangelo and Michelangelo has introduced them to his friend Rabbi Yehuda. William questions how a Christian monk and a Jewish rabbi could be friends. The rabbi responds sarcastically and laughs, but then gets serious and says that is it true, and that William would be fortunate to be in a friendship as good as that between Rabbi Yehuda and Michelangelo.

Before William can reply, Jeanne joins the conversation and says that William does have friends that good—two of them. William takes a deep breath, and then gets a little teary (p. 185).

The student stops talking. Bill gently asks why that moment is so important to her. The student replies that it seems to her that this is one of the most important parts of the book. William for the first time in his life has friends.

Bill says that this is an important thing to bring up. He asks why the student thinks it is so important to William to have friends. The student responds that maybe it is because William grew up with a bunch of monks. And that maybe William is getting emotional because he has been taught that Christians must stay away from Jews, who represent the Devil. And now that idea, which William probably always thought was wrong, has been shattered.

Bill says he is impressed with the secrets the students have discovered in their own readings of the text and he asks if anyone has any more. Another student volunteers. She starts off reading from her journal, but gradually speaks without referring to it.

She says it is easy, when reading the book, to forget that William is half-Saracen, and as a person of color and a person of mixed heritage, he is subject to prejudice. Even though he is a Christian monk in a society where Christians are dominant, his Saracen heritage makes people think he is Muslim. So even when there isn't direct prejudice, William has learned to expect it. Like when he meets Robert de Sorbonne, who is the president of a famous college. William expects to be asked about his Saracen heritage and, as a result, to lose any chance he might have for enrolling in the University even though he really wants to.

Instead, Robert de Sorbonne asks him an academic question, about what William thinks about Albertus's proof of the existence of God. William pauses, looking stunned. Jacob is afraid that William can't answer the question. Actually, though, William is stunned that Robert seems to be judging him by how smart he is, not by not by the color of his skin or his religion or culture. Robert misinterprets William's pause to mean that he does not know the answer. Then William asks which proof Robert means.

The student summarizing this scene smiles. She says that then it was Robert's turn to be confused. Robert clarifies that he is thinking of Albertus Magnus ... then William cuts him off and says of course he was talking about Albertus Magnus, but William wonders which of Albertus's two published proofs of the existence of God Robert is talking about.

Then William explains the proofs and Robert is impressed and says that he has a spot for William at the Sorbonne University and William is full of joy. And so, the student says, the secret is that the book doesn't say what William is happy about. Maybe it isn't just that he gets to go to college, maybe he is also happy because finally someone has seen him not as a Saracen, like those pilgrims saw him toward the beginning of the book, but as a monk who has studied really hard and is really smart and a good monk.

Another student asks if he can read a part in the book that he annotated. Bill encourages him to do so. This student wants to read the prayer that William says when they are about to rescue the books. The student reads the prayer from pages 259 and 260 that talks about how the children have tried to focus on God's voice in the midst of many other voices, both orthodox and allegedly heretical, from the powerful and the downtrodden, and even though it is had to make sense of it all, they have followed God's voice to the point in time where they now are. They ask God to hear them and help them as they face a bonfire of hate.

The student who read the prayer out loud says that William has gone from being happy that someone could see him as himself to a position where he is asking God to help them fight the flames of hate.

At this point, Bill enters the conversation. Though he usually stays quiet so that the students are the ones to bring forth ideas and insights, he makes it a practice to affirm the students' good work, by participating in the discussion as well. He also wants to highlight a passage that seems directly tied into the last student's words.

Bill directs the students' attentions to the end of the last chapter of the book. He flips to a marked page and describes the scene in which Jacob asks Michelangelo when their martyrdom will come. Earlier in the book, people kept calling the children saints, and Michelangelo has mentioned their martyrdom. Jacob doesn't seem scared when he asks the question even though he is talking about when they are going to be killed for their actions or beliefs. In response, Michelangelo asks William what the word *martyr* translates to in Latin, or in Greek. William says that, though his Greek is not so good, he knows that in Latin, the word means "Witness."

Michelangelo responds that William is right, and the children have already been witnesses to the goodness and beauty and justice of God. So, Michelangelo says that whether the children stay together or go in different directions, they will be witnesses to ignorance and fear, cruelty and hatred, as well as beauty and grace. And so, the children are martyrs—witnesses (p. 336).

Bill says the secret here is for the readers—that to make a difference in the world, people don't always have to give up their lives or fight a war or break laws, although he smiles and says there may be a place for that. He says it is important for the students to bear witness to things and to stand against ignorance and cruelty and for all that is beautiful in this broken world.

After a pause, Bill says to his students that he doesn't want to have the last word and asks if there is anyone else who could contribute a last secret that the text has revealed to them. He waits, letting the time stretch and put more pressure on the students, then a student volunteers.

The student points out that the class hasn't really talked about the Inquisitor, but that he makes a pilgrimage too. Bill asks him to elaborate. The student reminds the class that the Inquisitor remains in the background for the first three-quarters of the book. He asks for different people to tell the story of the children. He encourages each person to tell their tale and then he fades back. He really isn't even a character until chapter 23 (p. 278). In that chapter, the Inquisitor begins the narrating (p. 278).

He listens closely from the shadows and when the children speak of going to Mont-Saint-Michel the next day, he offers to lead them to there. The children agree and the Inquisitor comments that he wishes this had been his plan all along, but that sometimes God favors the fox over the rabbit (p. 289).

The student says that at this point in the book, he figured that the Inquisitor was going to be the villain for the big final fight at the end of the book. The student flips a couple of pages, then reads again, pointing out that the Inquisitor could be understood to be speaking with malice when he starts out describing William as looking like a very big child and Jacob as looking small and carefully aware of his surroundings. But then the Inquisitor's tone seems to change. He describes Jeanne as not resembling a sinful woman at all, in fact thinking of her that way is ridiculous. Then the Inquisitor admits that he would prefer to not kill them (p. 292).

But the student points out that another way to read the passage is that the Inquisitor is starting to think that the church might be wrong about suspecting and fearing these children who seem so innocent.

The student turns more pages. The children are talking, and the Inquisitor finds himself saying more than he planned. He talks to the children about how, on one hand, Jesus told his people to love God with all their hearts. That makes sense to him, but then Jesus says the second greatest commandment is to love your neighbor as yourself. And that doesn't make sense to him. He doesn't understand how loving God, a perfect, divine, and faithful being, could be the same as loving your flawed and broken neighbor. The inquisitor doesn't understand how that is possible (p. 296).

And then, the student says, the Inquisitor tells the children he is Etienne of Arles, the youngest son of a rich family. While his brothers became knights, he became a scholar and the Pope invited him to become an Inquisitor. He fell in love with a woman, violated his vows, and was told that if he had any more trouble he would be defrocked and kicked out of the Inquisitors. He was then assigned to investigate the children. He tells them that once he investigated, he found the story was not as simple as it seemed. He started to think that maybe the Church was wrong, that maybe the Pope was wrong. He decides that the children are not the center of some evil cult; they are not heretics. He believes in them. He believes that they are saints (p. 300).

He then takes out a knife. He aims it at them. The children are frightened. And the student says that he figured there would be a big fight with William wrestling the guy to the ground. Instead, Etienne continues in what sounds like a rant.

The students describes Etienne trying to work out his options. He could go back to Rome and tell his superiors that the children he was sent to investigate are all saints—but that wouldn't help him at all. The church officials would take over and Etienne would be pushed into the background. But if the children are martyred, if they die, and if Etienne can take possession of their bones, then the bones will perform miracles and Etienne can witness the miracles and then he can be important as the curator of their holy relics.

Etienne goes on like that for a while, the student explains, standing, the knife gripped in his hand. He turns the knife around so that it is in a stabbing position. Then he stabs the knife into the dirt. He admits he cannot do it (p. 301).

He confesses that he wanted to. He says he was wrong. He falls to the ground, weeping. And it is Jeanne who puts her hand on his back and comforts him and tells him that they forgive him.

The student says, "So that is a pilgrimage, right? I mean, like he learned about the children, he was set to kill them and then he didn't and they forgave him. That is a pretty major transformation." Bill confirms that it is both a transformation and a pilgrimage, then wraps up the session.

CAN TEACHERS REALLY EXPECT TO GET QUALITY RESPONSES TO YA LITERATURE USING PaRDeS?

This chapter strings together responses from multiple classrooms and often different class periods focusing on different sections of the book. And while it does skip over the disruptions, false starts, and the struggles to get responses that are a natural part of high school teaching, all of these responses are possible. There are, however, some caveats:

1. Students get better at responding to sacred text techniques the more experience they have with them. A teacher who uses each technique once in a semester is less likely to see rich discussions than a teacher who comes back to an approach multiple times.
2. Students need time to read the book. Students who have not read the book will confine themselves to shallow and short responses. If they know an in-depth discussion through PaRDeS is coming, there is a

reason to read the book. We recommend that teachers use a lot of reading aloud and in-class reading with the first book of the semester. Once the students have experienced an in-depth discussion, the teacher can gradually transition to more reading-as-homework if they wish.
3. The reason that PaRDeS and other sacred text techniques work is that instead of starting out a discussion by taking a broad view and, for example, asking students what themes they noticed, or worse, outlining the themes for them, all of these sacred text techniques start by looking at a very small, very concrete passage. This makes clear to the students that the teacher cares about specific passages and the students will respond in kind.
4. Focusing on specific passages can also strengthen the connections between passages and students' contexts, without as many lengthy stories from the students' lives that have only a tenuous connection to the literature that the class is studying.

In conclusion, as we have said multiple times in this book, these techniques can be used with other books, and the books we have mentioned include multiple ways in which they can be seen as prayers by the authors. The final chapter will give more detail on this. But rest assured, using sacred text approaches can deepen the quality of your student's responses.

Conclusion

Closing Our Discussion and the Books

As authors of this book, we have some commonalities that connect us and drive our work together. For one, our group shares a deep love for stories and particularly for young adult literature, first and foremost as readers but also as teachers and teacher educators. We love the way stories point us to something bigger than ourselves and place our experiences and feelings within a framework that extends beyond our individual experiences and beyond what we can see. We love the ways that literature conveys fundamental human truths and questions that can't be otherwise explained or described. The books we've featured in our chapters are some of our favorites.

Also, we're committed to a faith tradition. This looks different for each of us. We each express and live out our beliefs differently but across these differences is our shared commitment to our religious and spiritual convictions, traditions, rhythms, and practices. Out of this is another shared commitment to acknowledge, value, and support our students' religious and spiritual identities, whatever these may be.

Our love for young adult (YA) literature and our commitments to our own faith and others' have not always overlapped. We have noticed a lack of YA scholarship focusing on religion or faith. What scholarship we found tended to focus on overt or explicit mention of religion or religious themes. We understand why. Fear of offending or isolating readers makes sense to us.

And yet, open discussions of ethical and moral dilemmas and situations are exactly what we think YA books are able to do so well with readers and in classroom settings. We believe that YA novels are particularly well positioned to illustrate the ways characters grow and change, and to explore faith-related questions and situations from a variety of viewpoints.

In our work together over the years, we've experimented with different ways to approach YA literature through the lens of religious and spiritual development. We've presented at various national conferences and have received valuable feedback from teachers, researchers, teacher educators, and authors themselves. This feedback and our continued reading, thinking, and discussing prompted us to land on the framework you've seen here in these pages. It's our hope that you find it as generative and helpful as we do.

Rather than focusing on how often or accurately a religious or spiritual experience is portrayed, we offer an approach that opens wide the possibilities for thinking about and discussing with others spiritual and faith-based themes in YA literature. We hope that this has been the case throughout our chapters. We believe it's important to consider the whole of the story, looking at setting, characters, themes, and point of view and the ways they all contribute.

We've avoided, for example, looking at explicitly religious symbols or characters and, instead, examine how protagonists grow in terms of their relationships to others and how they became aware of something transcendent that they could connect with. Our approach doesn't center the characters' spiritual or religious development or exploration, but foregrounds readers' own yearnings, hopes, convictions, and beliefs as they consider how spiritual and faith-based themes permeate the entire context of books.

It's our hope that by considering each book as a type of prayer that the book offers the world—more than a theme, but a way of speaking to something beyond human experience—about human experience—might open up new ways of thinking about YA literature. This is particularly important during a time when some groups of people seek to censor the books children read in school. In case after case, the reasoning for banning the books is based on reading small—looking only at a particular character, paragraph, or even sentence. Reading the entire book as an expression of lament, confession, equanimity, pilgrimage, anger, or joy helps us to see beyond the mundane to the larger moral issues and ethical questions the book raises.

This approach also encourages a broader interpretive range of responses that go beyond moral agnosticism, partisan divisiveness, power differentials, didacticism, and theological evaluation. As we've mentioned earlier, this approach does not assume authors' intent. Because our approach foregrounds readers' experience and their commitments, values, or beliefs, authors' spiritual or religious commitments aren't paramount. In fact, our approach doesn't even require that faith or religion is even explicitly addressed. A book may reflect the reader's prayer of anger, or a partner group's understanding of thankfulness, or a classroom's expression of yearning for a less-violent world.

This said, we realize that our approach might not work or be as effective with all YA literature. We recognize that some books are primarily for enjoyment, and we think that is okay. Some books reach inside of us and make clear that which we could not express. Others offer us a roller coaster adventure, or a quiet story of beauty, or a good laugh. And all those are excellent ways to enjoy a book too.

Key to our approach is an understanding of prayer that might push our readers past more narrow definitions of what prayer is and does. Thinking about YA novels through a lens of prayer as guttural and personal utterances in response to a universe that spans the emotional landscape is, perhaps, a new way for many of our readers to think about prayer. Santa Claus letter-lists of wants, public performative prayers that sound inauthentic, or rote prayers that are void of any personal meaning are much more common (and often negative) understandings of prayer.

Our approach to prayer as expressions of praise, yearning, lament, anger, confession, reconciliation, obedience, meditation, and contemplation, joy, desire for equanimity and thankfulness, pilgrimage, and other ideas, opens up new possibilities for connection across faith traditions and religious or spiritual commitments.

Our list of prayers isn't meant to be exhaustive, and we encourage our readers to think of and use other prayers with our approach. We also think the same book could be read through the lens of more than one prayer. This is exciting to us as we believe there's something elusive about the themes in books and the ways these themes are carried throughout them. For example, here's a list of other kinds of prayers that we think could also be applied to the books we've discussed.

- *Internment* (Samira Ahmed): Anger, Yearning
- *The Hate U Give* (Angie Thomas): Anger, Lament
- *Long Way Down* (Jason Reynolds): Anger, Lament, Yearning, Contemplation
- *Speak* (Laurie Halse Anderson): Anger, Lament, Contemplation
- *Goodbye Days* (Jeff Zetner): Lament, Reconciliation, Thankfulness
- *brown girl dreaming* (Jacqueline Woodson): Pilgrimage, Joy
- *The War That Saved My Life* (Kimberly Brubaker Bradley): Yearning, Anger, Lament
- *The Poet X* (Elizabeth Acevdeo): Anger, Yearning, Obedience
- *Louisiana's Way Home* (Kate DiCamillo): Pilgrimage, Yearning, Joy
- *Orbiting Jupiter* (Gary Schmidt): Anger, Yearning
- *Beast Player* (Nahoko Uehashi): Obedience, Contemplation
- *Where the Mountain Meets the Moon* (Grace Lin): Yearning, Thankfulness
- *The Fault in Our Stars* (John Green): Anger, Yearning, Thankfulness, Pilgrimage
- *The Inquisitor's Tale* (Adam Gidwitz): Joy, Reconciliation

Through we focused on 15 books, here are some suggestions for other books to use for each one of the prayers we discuss:

Here is a initial list to get you started:

- **Anger:** *Between Shades of Gray* (Ruta Sepetys), *Children of Blood and Bone* (Tomi Adeyemi), *March* Series (John Lewis, Andrew Aydin, and Nate Powell), *The Girl Who Drank the Moon* (Kelly Barnhill), *Long Way Down* (Jason Reynolds)
- **Yearning:** *Strange the Dreamer* (Laini Taylor), *Vincent and Theo* (Deborah Heiligman), *Eleanor and Park* (Rainbow Rowell), *The Graveyard Book* (Neil Gaiman), *Kira Kira* (Cynthia Kadohata), *In Darkness* (Nick Lake), *The Book Thief* (Markus Zusak) *Just Like That* (Gary Schmidt), *Extremely Loud and Incredibly Close* (Jonathan Safran Foer), *Dig* (A. S. King)
- **Contemplation:** *The Serpent King* (Jeff Zetner), *Crossover* (Kwame Alexander), *We Are Okay* (Nina LaCour), *Just Like That* (Gary Schmidt), *Extremely Loud and Incredibly Close* (Jonathan Safran Foer)
- **Confession:** *Scythe* (Neal Shusterman), *Dig* (A. S. King), *Kira Kira* (Cynthia Kadohata), *Belles* Series (Dhonielle Clayton)
- **Reconciliation:** *Crossover* (Kwame Alexander), *Dragon Hoops* (Gene Luen Yang), *Dig* (A. S. King), *Kira Kira* (Cynthia Kadohata), *Just Like That* (Gary Schmidt), *The War I Finally Won* (Kimberly Brubaker Bradley)
- **Equanimity:** *The Graveyard Book* (Neil Gaiman), *Dig* (A. S. King) *The War I Finally Won* (Kimberly Brubaker Bradley)
- **Thankfulness:** *Ordinary Hazards* (Nikki Grimes), *The Girl Who Drank the Moon* (Kelly Barnhill), *The War I Finally Won* (Kimberly Brubaker Bradley), *Just Like That* (Gary Schmidt)
- **Obedience:** *Dragon Hoops* (Gene Luen Yang), *Children of Blood and Bone* (Tomi Adeyemi), *Navigating Early* (Clare Vanderpool)
- **Pilgrimage:** *Children of Blood and Bone* (Tomi Adeyemi), *Ready Player One* (Ernest Cline), *Navigating Early* (Clare Vanderpool), *Ordinary Hazards* (Nikki Grimes), *Firekeepers Daughter* (Angeline Boulley)
- **Lament:** *Between Shades of Gray* (Ruta Sepetys), *Scythe* (Neal Shusterman), *Dragon Hoops* (Gene Luen Yang), *Dig* (A. S. King), *March* Series (Andrew Aydin and John Lewis)
- **Joy:** *Between Shades of Gray* (Ruta Sepetys), *The Sun Is Also A Star* (Nicola Yoon), *The Girl Who Drank the Moon* (Kelly Barnhill)

In our framework, we offer practical and specific suggestions for how to approach YA literature as prayers and so we encourage using the interpretive practices that we've outlined and described throughout the book: Lectio

Divina, PaRDeS, Ignatian Spirituality, havruta, marginalia, florilegium. These approaches avoid a didactic approach whereby students might be told how to read or think about a book's meaning, character development, or overall themes.

These practices recognize that a good book is interwoven in such a way that each sentence provides a point of entrée to discuss the overall messages the book carries. These practices also approach the text as being sacred, as having something relevant and meaningful to say to us. Those specific words, phrases, sentences and paragraphs, in discussion with other readers, can illuminate and clarify moments in readers' own lives. Through the use of interpretive practices, readers and teachers can approach a book in nuanced ways that make space for multiple points of view from characters and the readers themselves.

While some or all of these interpretive practices might be new to our readers, we think they are helpful and productive beyond the connections to religion and spirituality that we discuss. In fact, we think they could be used to support many statewide or national English Language Arts secondary standards focused on literature, close reading, and making connections to texts. There is indeed overlap between the practices we've described here and the well-known and commonly used text to self, text to text, and text to world strategies.

However, we think these practices also open up new possibilities for how to respond to literature. Using these practices can acknowledge, affirm, and build on the religious literacy practices that our students might already participate in. They provide a broader vocabulary and specific methods for thinking about and discussing moral, ethical, spiritual, or religious dimensions of stories as well as the ethical or moral dilemmas within them. Approaching YA literature as prayers allows space to unpack, explore, and reflect upon issues of justice, rightness and wrongness, meaning, calling, and transcendence.

References

Acevedo, E. (2018). *The poet X: A novel*. New York: HarperTeen.
Ahmed, Samira. (2019). *Internment*. New York: Little, Brown.
Augustine, of Hippo. (1992). *Confessions of St. Augustine*. Oxford: Oxford University Press.
Betzalel, N., & Schechtman, Z. (2017). The impact of bibliotherapy superheroes on youth who experience parental absence. *School Psychology International, 38*(5), 473–90.
Bonhoeffer, D. (1939). *Life together*. New York: HarperOne.
Bradley, Kimberly Brubaker. (2015). *The war that saved my life*. New York: Dial.
Bussing, A., Ostermann, T., & Matthiessen, P. (2006). Distinct expressions of vital spirituality. *Journal of Religion & Health, 46*(2), 267–86.
Catalano, A. (2008). Making a place on the shelves of a curriculum materials center: The case for helping pre-service teachers use developmental bibliotherapy in the classroom. Education Libraries, *31*(1). https://doi.org/10.26443/el.v31i3.258
Centers for Disease Control and Prevention. (2013, May 17). Mental health surveillance among children—United States, 2005–2011. *Morbidity and Mortality Weekly Report, 60*(2), 1–35.
Collins, Billy. Poemhunter. https://www.poemhunter.com/poem/marginalia/.
Daniels, H., Zemelman, S., & Steineke, N. (2007). *Content-area writing: Every teacher's guide*. Portsmouth, NH: Heinemann.
Deitcher, H. (2019). Bibliotherapy and teaching Jewish texts: "Medicine for the mind." *Religious Education, 114*(1), 17–29.
DiCamillo, K. (2018). *Louisiana's way home*. Somerville, MA: Candlewick Press, 2018.
Farb, N. A. S., Anderson, A. K., & Segal, Z. V. (2012). The mindful brain and emotion regulation in mood disorders. *Canadian Journal of Psychiatry, 57*(2), 70–77.
Filmer-Davies, C. (1997) Presence and absence: God in fantasy literature. *Christianity and Literature* 47 (1) 59–74.
Flood, G. (1996). *An introduction to Hinduism*. Cambridge: Cambridge University Press.

Ford, D. Y., McZeal Walters, N., Byrd, J. A., & Harris, B.N. (2018). I want to read about me: Engaging and empowering gifted black girls using multicultural literature and bibliotherapy. *Gifted Child Today, 42* (1), 53–57.
Foster, R. J. (1978). *Celebration of discipline*. San Francisco: HarperOne.
Gidwitz, Adam. (2016). *The inquisitor's tale*. New York: Dutton.
Green, J. (2012). *The fault in our stars*. New York: Penguin Group.
Halse Anderson, L. (2018). *Speak: The graphic novel*. New York: Farrar Straus Giroux Books for Young Readers.
Hebert, T. & Furner, J. (1997). Helping high ability students overcome math anxiety through bibliotherapy. *Journal of Secondary Gifted Education, 8*(4), 164–78. https://www.contemplative.org/contemplative-practice/lectio-divina/.
Joubert, C., & Hay, J. (2019). Capacitating postgraduate education students with lay counseling competencies via the culturally appropriate bibliotherapeutic Read-me-to-Resilience intervention. *South African Journal of Education, 39*(3), 1–13.
Koubovi, D. (1970). *Therapeutic teaching: Teaching contents as a means for improving mental health* (Hebrew). Jerusalem: Hebrew University of Jerusalem.
Larsen, J. (2017). *Movies are prayers: How films voice our deepest longings*. Downers Grove, Illinois: IVP Books.
Lin, G. (2019). *Where the mountain meets the moon*. New York: Little, Brown Books for Young Readers.
Lee, N.C. (2010). Lament in the Bible and in music and poetry across cultures today. *IBL Teaching the Bible: An e-newsletter for public school teachers by Society of Biblical Literature*, February.
Leibowitz, N. (1941). He'erot metodiyot l'limud chumash im mefarshim b'beit hasefer hatichoni' (Hebrew). *Hed Hinuch*.
Lenkowsky, R. (1987). Bibliotherapy: A review and analysis of the literature. *The Journal of Special Education, 21*(2), 123–32.
Lewis. C. S. (1966). *The weight of glory*. New York: Macmillan and Co.
Linton, M., & Koonmen, J. (2020). Self-care as an ethical obligation for nurses. *Nursing Ethics, 27*(8), 1694–1702.
Lutovac, S., & Kasila, R. (2020). How to select reading for application of pedagogical bibliotherapy? Insights from prospective teachers' identification processes. *Journal of Mathematics Teacher Education, 23*, 483–98.
Mann, G. (2020). Emptiness, equanimity, and the self object function. *Psychoanalytic Inquiry: A Topical Journal for Mental Health Professionals, 40*(5), 300–10.
Marginalia. OED Online, Oxford: Oxford University Press. www.oed.com/viewdictionaryentry/Entry/11125.
Mason, E. (2016). Punctive grace: Reading religion in Barthes' *Mourning Diary*. *Textual Practice, 30*(2), 327–43.
McCulloch, R. (2021). Accessing the wisdom of the body: Somatic transformation of OD practitioners. *Organization of Development Review, 53*(2), 83–90.
McKillop, H. (2020). Harry Potter and the creation of spiritual technologies. Master's thesis, University of Ottawa. https://ruor.uottawa.ca/bitstream/10393/41019/3/Mckillop_Hannah_2020_thesis.pdf.

McMahon, M. (2021). Inshaallah. https://www.wisegeek.com/what-does-inshaallah-mean.htm.

National Center for Children in Poverty. (2014). *Children's mental health*. New York: Columbia University, Mailman School of Public Health, Department of Health Policy & Management.

Nicholson, J., & Pearson, Q. (2003). Helping children cope with fears: Using children's literature in classroom guidance. *Professional School Counseling, 7*, 15–19.

Nickerson, A., & Hinton, D. E. (2011). Anger regulation in traumatized Cambodian refugees: The perspectives of Buddhist monks. *Culture, Medicine and Psychiatry, 35*(3), 396–416.

Oxford English dictionary (Online ed.). Oxford University Press.

Rawls, G., Clark, D., & Hall, S. (2020). Bibliotherapy and group counseling with African-American college students: A case study approach. *Journal for Specialists in Group Work, 43*(5), 242–56.

Reddy, S. D., Negi, L. T., Dodson-Lavelle, B., Ozawa-de Silva, B., Pace, T. W., & Craighead, L. W. (2013). Cognitive-based compassion training: A promising prevention strategy for at-risk adolescents. *Journal of Child and Family Studies, 22*(2), 219–230.

Reynolds, J. (2017). *Long way down: The graphic novel*. New York: Atheneum.

Rittel, H. W., & Webber, M. M. (1973). Dilemmas in a general theory of planning. *Policy Sciences, 4*(2), 155–69.

Rosenblatt, Louise M. (1968). *Literature as exploration*. Noble & Noble.

Sauter, G. (2005). Reconciliation. In E. Fahlbusch, J. M. Lochman, J. Mbiti, J. Pelikan, & L. Vischer (eds.), *The Encyclopedia of Christianity*, vol. 4, pp. 504–6. Leiden: Brill.

Schat, Sean. (2020). The successful communication of educational care. In Paul Shotsberger and Cathy Freytag, *How Then Shall We Care?* Eugene, OR: Wipf & Stock.

Schmidt, Gary. (2017). *Orbiting Jupiter*. New York: Houghton Mifflin.

Sims, Bishop, R. (1990). Mirrors, windows, and sliding glass doors. *Perspectives, 1*(3), ix–xi.

Thomas, Angie. (2017). *The hate U give*. New York: Beltzer and Bray.

Tijms, J., Stoop, M., & Polleck, J. (2018). Bibliotherapeutic book club intervention to promote reading skills and social-emotional competenices in low SES community-based high schools: A randomized controlled trial. *Journal of Research in Reading, 41*(3), 525–45.

Uehashi, Nahoko. (2019). *The beast player*. New York: Henry Holt.

Understanding Anger. University Health Services, University of California, Berkeley. https://uhs.berkeley.edu/sites/default/files/understanding_anger_0.pdf.

Weber, J. (2019). Mindful of equanimity. *The Psychologist*. April letters.

Weber, J. (2021). A systematic literature review of equanimity in mindfulness-based interventions. *Pastoral Psychology, 70*, 151–65.

Williams. H. A. (2009). *Self-taught: African American education in slavery and freedom*. Chapel Hill: University of North Carolina Press.

Woodson, Jacqueline. (2014). *brown girl dreaming*. New York: Penguin.

Zentner, Jeff. (2017). *Goodbye days*. New York: Crown.

Zoltan, V. (2021). *Praying with Jane Eyre*: *Reflections on reading as a sacred practice*. New York: TarcherPerigee.

Zoltan, V., & ter Kuile, C. (2020). *Harry Potter and the Sacred Text.* Podcast.

Zoran, R. (2000). *The third voice* (Hebrew). Jerusalem: Carmel Publishers.

Index

Acevedo, Elizabeth, 81, 149
Ahmed, Samira, xvii, 1, 149
Anderson, Laurie Halse, 23–24, 149
The Beast Player, 93–94, 100–108, 149

bibliotherapy, 27–30
Bishop, Rudine Sims, 27
Bradley, Kimberly Brubaker, 65, 149
Bridge to Terabithia, xii
Brown, Michael, 19
brown girl dreaming, 51–54, 149
Browne, Sir Thomas, xi
Buber, Martin, xiv

Caritas as element of equanimity, 57–59
Catcher in the Rye, xi
Cisneros, Ernesto, xii
contemplation, 111–113

Dante, xi
DiCamillo, Kate, 81, 149
Dickens, Charles, xi

equanimity, 51–52, 54–59

The Fault in Our Stars, 119–128, 149
florilegium, 1, 7–12, 119, 125–127
Forster, E. M., x–xi

Geisel, Theodore ("Dr. Seuss"), xii
Gidwitz, Adam, 129, 149
Goodbye Days, 35–50, 149
Green, John, xiii, 120, 149
guilt, 37–41

Harry Potter and the Sacred Text podcast, xvii
The Hate U Give, xvii, 14–21
havruta, discussion practice of, 52, 59–64, 93–107
Hollow Horn, John, 3
Homer, xi

Ignatian imagery, 49–50
The Inquisitor's Tale, 129–145, 149
Internment, xvii, 1–12, 149

Jones, Tom, xi

King, Dr. Martin Luther, Jr., 20

Larsen, Josh, xvi, 109, 129
lectio divina, 19–21, 76–78
Lee, Nancy, 3, 5
Lewis, C. S., 14
Lewis, John, Senator, 20
Lin, Grace, 110–111, 149

Long Way Down, 23, 25–26, 28, 30–34, 149
Louisiana's Way Home, 81–85, 149

marginalia discussion technique, 89–91, 116–118
Martin, Trayvon, 16
Merton, Thomas, 111–112
Myers, Walter Dean, *Monster*, xiii

Orbiting Jupiter, 93–100, 104, 107–108, 149

PaRDeS approach to discussion, 31–33, 129–146
Parks, Rosa, 20
The Poet X, 81–82, 85–89, 149
Prayer of Anger, 23–34
Prayer of Confession, 35–50
Prayer of Joy, 119–128
Prayer of Lament, 3–6
Prayer of Obedience, 93–108
Prayer of Thankfulness, 65–79
Prayer of Yearning, 13–21
prayers, xvi

Rabbi Israel of Rizhyn, ix–x, xiii
Rabbi Moshe of Kobryn, ix–x
Reynolds, Jason, xii, 23, 25, 149

Rice, Tamir, 19

Schat, Sean, 68
Schmidt, Gary, ix–xiii, 93–94, 149
Silf, Margaret, 109
Speak: The Graphic Novel, 23–25, 28, 30–34, 149

Ter Kuile, Casper, xvi, 89
Thomas, Angie, xvii, 14, 149
Tolkien, J. R. R., 14
trauma, 26–34

Uehashi, Nohoko, 93–94, 149

Wagner, Richard, xi
The War That Saved My Life, 65–79, 149
Webster, John, xi
Where the Mountain Meets the Moon, 109–118, 149
Wilder, Thornton, xii
Woodson, Jacqueline, xii, 51–54, 149
Wordsworth, William, 109
Write Around activity, 90–91

Zentner, Jeff, 35, 149
Zimmerman, George, 16
Zoltan, Vanessa, xvii, 89, 130–131

About the Authors

William Boerman-Cornell is a Professor of Education and English at Trinity Christian College, located just south and west of Chicago. He has co-authored two previous books, both about using graphic novels in middle school and high school classrooms. When he isn't teaching, reading, writing, or grading papers, he enjoys biking, hiking, canoeing, exploring neighborhoods, and engaging in competitive sand sculpture. He lives with his family about 20 minutes from the Loop.

Deborah Vriend Van Duinen, an Associate Professor of English Education at Hope College in Holland, Michigan, teaches and researches adolescent literacy and young adult literature which means she gets to read a lot of books and think and write about them. She directs Hope College's NEA Big Read Lakeshore, an annual month-long community-wide reading program. Deb loves adventuring with her family in beautiful West Michigan, her beloved homeland of Canada, and the world.

Kristine Alatheia Mensonides Gritter is the chair of the Literacy, Language, & Equity program at Seattle Pacific University and a professor. She is interested in literature and literary discussions that offer deeper insights to students and has written several articles and one book on the topic. She tends to read in spurts when she discovers an author she really likes. She also enjoys murder-mystery shows. She suggests that mystery readers "Look at the in-laws before you look at the outlaws."

Xu Bian is an Assistant Professor in Seattle Pacific University's Department of Languages, Cultures, and Linguistics, located on the hills of beautiful Seattle, Washington. She has publications in the field of Young Adult literature, foreign language acquisition, and teaching. She likes to travel, swim, hike around Seattle and the rest of the planet, camp, and play piano in her spare time. Her co-authors think that her knowledge, kindness, and humility know no bounds.

www.ingramcontent.com/pod-product-compliance
Lightning Source LLC
Chambersburg PA
CBHW020125240426
43673CB00038B/594